consider the lilies

a

take up & READ

publication

In memory of Michael Greiner,
who heard and answered the call to take up and read every day.

Editorial Director: Elizabeth Foss
Designed by: Emma Catarino
Editors: Carly Buckholz, Katy Greiner, and Irene Starrs
Cover Art: Kristin Foss
Calligraphy: Claire Craig

ISBN-13: 978-1547239481
ISBN-10: 1547239484

Welcome!

Maybe this is a hard season in your life—you're overwhelmed by the burdens weighing you down, the crosses that He's asked you to carry. You look heavenward and all you feel is… abandoned.

This study is for you.

It is full of the consolations of the Holy Spirit. Here, you will find a guidebook to what God is saying, how He is encouraging you to lament, to pour out your grief and your fears and your anger. This journal acknowledges that in this broken, fallen world we do suffer.

Or maybe you're in a sweet spot. Life is really rather good right now. You're not feeling any particular strain.

This study is for you, too.

In it, you find the words you need to console a friend, to empathize with the people around you who are suffering. I promise you, they *are* suffering. You are daily surrounded by people who bow low under the weight of grief, often without any outward sign of dismay. This study makes you a better friend to the woman next to you, to the growing child who aches, to the spouse who despairs. And it buries words into your heart so that they are there, waiting, when the rain begins to fall. Because it will fall.

This study is for all of us. We're all in it together.

Finally, while it is our hearts' desire and firm conviction that the words in this journal will be a balm to the heart of every woman, we also want you to know that we are acutely aware that there is a serious difference between praying through the ups and downs and daily worries of life and the battle with clinical anxiety, depression, and mental illness. In no way do we intend to diminish that struggle by implying that if you just pray enough with these words, all will be well. If you are managing mental illness through medication and professional therapeutic help, then we hope you will allow these pages to be another tool in your arsenal, a light that shines to remind you that you are not alone in the dark. But they should not be considered a substitute for professional mental health care. If you have not been clinically diagnosed with depression or anxiety, but find yourself questioning the possibility, or feel that your struggles with anxiety or dark times are affecting your life daily, we strongly encourage you to tell someone you love, ask for help, and seek a professional evaluation. Your Father desires your wholeness above all else, and so do we. You never walk alone!

With Love,
Elizabeth Foss and the Take Up and Read Team

Keep in Touch!

On the Web
www.takeupandread.org

Share your journal pictures and help us find you: #considerthelilies2017

Instagram
@takeupandread

Twitter
@totakeupandread

Facebook
Find us on FaceBook at Take Up and Read

PSALM 56:1-4 (NRSV-CE)

Be gracious to me, O God, for people trample on me;
   all day long foes oppress me;
my enemies trample on me all day long,
   for many fight against me.
O Most High, when I am afraid,
   I put my trust in you.
In God, whose word I praise,
   in God I trust; I am not afraid;
   what can flesh do to me?

JOHN 17:11-19 (NRSV-CE)

And now I am no longer in the world, but they are in the world, and I am coming to you. Holy Father, protect them in your name that you have given me, so that they may be one, as we are one. While I was with them, I protected them in your name that you have given me. I guarded them, and not one of them was lost except the one destined to be lost, so that the scripture might be fulfilled. But now I am coming to you, and I speak these things in the world so that they may have my joy made complete in themselves. I have given them your word, and the world has hated them because they do not belong to the world, just as I do not belong to the world. I am not asking you to take them out of the world, but I ask you to protect them from the evil one. They do not belong to the world, just as I do not belong to the world. Sanctify them in the truth; your word is truth. As you have sent me into the world, so I have sent them into the world. And for their sakes I sanctify myself, so that they also may be sanctified in truth.

For further reading: John 15: 7-11, John 16:1-4

THINK UPON THESE THINGS

The day I learned that it just was not feasible to publish in this journal all the Bible verses we've found for you—all the words of consolation and comfort and compassion—I admit I cried. Sacred Scripture. His words. That was the whole point. What is this book without all those words?

It is an invitation. It is an opportunity to take up and read your own Bible.

It is Wednesday of Holy Week as I write these words. With the universal Church, I prepare for the Triduum, knowing that the next three days will make me painfully aware that Jesus died and left this earth, left us. We didn't walk with Him on dusty roads. We didn't break bread with Him in the upper room. We didn't hear His voice as he spoke the Sermon on the Mount. He suffered and died long before we were born.

In those hours before He died, Jesus knew His friends would be without Him soon, and He knew that we'd never have the advantage of looking Him in the eyes and sitting at His feet. He very purposefully provided for us. Jesus left His Spirit to sustain the apostles in every conceivable trial. And He left us the same strength and grace. By the work of the Holy Spirit, through the careful stewardship of the Church, He provided words that promise joy and peace. When we falter and stumble and begin to doubt, He reminds us in His Word that His voice can be wholeheartedly believed. Every one of God's promises is to be trusted, and we can shout a resounding "Amen!" to His glory (see 2 Corinthians 1:20).

As you work your way through this journal for the next six weeks, our dearest hope is that you will grow to love—to crave—the feel of the weight of His Word on your lap. We want you to look forward with eager joy to opening that blessed book every day and pulling your pen across its heart, drawing the message into your heart.

I wanted the verses all here for you. God wants something more. He wants a real and very personal relationship with only you in your own personal copy of the Sacred Scripture. He wants you to seek Him and He wants to be found. He wants intimacy. He wants a long-term relationship. He wants to show you how His Word endures. The living Jesus wants you to begin to see that, even over a lifetime, He is unchanging, reliable, and utterly trustworthy. He wants you to look up all the verses under "For Further Reading" and let them lead you where He intends you to go.

Catholics know Scripture. We hear it corporately; it is beautifully woven throughout our liturgies. This is right and good and holy. But there is more. There is the personal conversation Jesus wants to have with you in the quiet of the morning, while you sit curled up on the corner of your couch wearing your pjs. He left His words for those moments, too. Those bedhead, been up all night, don't know how I'm going to do this day moments. He's there, waiting. He left His words for the random Tuesday afternoon when the rejection letter comes. He left them for the bedside vigil as you watch your mother slip from this life. He left them so you could celebrate and sing praises with Him while you admire a shiny new ring on your left hand, and then while you learn the fine art of nursing a baby while reading a book. He wants to speak into your soul every day, all day long.

Approach your Bible with reverent joy. Ask the Holy Spirit into your reading. The Church reminds us that time with the Word is time in prayer.

"…Prayer should accompany the reading of Sacred Scripture, so that God and man may talk together; for "we speak to Him when we pray; we hear Him when we read the divine saying" (Dei Verbum, 25).

So, open your Bible and leave it open. Find these verses every day and make them yours. Then, revisit your own Bible again and again. Don't be afraid to get splatters from the stove on its pages because you're refreshing real paper pages as you stir spaghetti. Don't be afraid to write or draw or even paint in it, if that's how you speak best. Acquire the habit of all-day, every day dialogue with God. This is our hope and prayer for you.

More importantly, this is what Jesus wants.

Elizabeth Foss

TO PONDER WITH YOUR PEN

What Bible will you use for this study? Put it with this journal and some pens that work in your Bible, in a place where you will find it again and again throughout the day. Open it today and find the verses at the top of this page. Underline them in your Bible. Choose a couple to copy below. Begin to write Sacred Scripture into your heart.

_____

_____

_____

_____

_____

_____

_____

_____

_____

_____

_____

_____

_____

_____

_____

_____

LIFTED TO THE LORD

Please, God, inspire in me an ever-deepening love for You in the Word.

PHILIPPIANS 4: 4-9 (NRSV-CE)

Rejoice in the Lord always; again I will say, Rejoice. Let your gentleness be known to everyone. The Lord is near. Do not worry about anything, but in everything by prayer and supplication with thanksgiving let your requests be made known to God. And the peace of God, which surpasses all understanding, will guard your hearts and your minds in Christ Jesus.

Finally, beloved, whatever is true, whatever is honorable, whatever is just, whatever is pure, whatever is pleasing, whatever is commendable, if there is any excellence and if there is anything worthy of praise, think about these things. Keep on doing the things that you have learned and received and heard and seen in me, and the God of peace will be with you.

For further reading: Habakkuk 3:17-19

THINK UPON THESE THINGS

It was not my intent to begin this study with these verses. I planned to meet you where you might be—discouraged, worried, perhaps even depressed. I wanted to put my arm around your shoulders and tell you I understand. I was going to share with you that I struggle with anxiety and depression, that I fight every day to keep them at bay. The first installment here was to be one of sitting with you in the pain, lamenting together.

I hear your groaning; I really do. I empathize and I am very much with you in your sorrows, whether they are fleeting for the day or they linger over months and seasons.

But we begin with rejoicing. We begin with the call to give thanks in all circumstances and to rejoice in the Lord always. Instead of beginning with a sorrowful stumble through the valley and then climbing to the height of rejoicing, we are going to begin with songs of praise.

Anxiety is the paralyzing fear that the next bad thing is going to happen. Perhaps we've lived a stretch of bad things and we're conditioned to look around corners expectantly, guarding against the next one. Perhaps there's no logical reason we're wired to expect grief; the expectation just comes upon us stealthily, darkening our days and quickening our heart rates. Regardless of the origin, most people suffer fear and sorrow to one degree or another.

The antidote to our afflictions is God. Jesus entered into this world of pain and He made an audacious promise: *It's all going to be just fine. Better than fine, really. It's all going to be fabulous.* He tells us straight up "do not worry about your life, what you will eat, or about your body, what you will wear" (Luke 12:22). *I'm God. I've got this.*

Some days, I weep and wail at the seeming absurdity of His simplistic assurances. Just don't worry. Just let it go and let God have full control. It's not that simple, is it? I came wired with an active imagination, a temperament prone to anxiety, and a very troubled childhood from which to draw anxious conclusions about life itself. I came with a hyperactive mind—and it goes a hundred miles an hour in the wrong direction.

Anxiety wants to dialogue with me. God wants my full attention. Anxiety wants me to dwell in the what-if scenario, the story I'm telling myself about the worst outcome. God wants me to recount the blessings He has bestowed on me and focus on His promises. It's a battle to see who captures my thoughts: the evil one with his evil technicolor fears or the Lord of the universe with His faithful promises.

We begin here. On the battleground. One of the choicest weapons is the gratitude record in the back of this journal. There, every day for the next six weeks, you will record three blessings. Just three—but three every day. Faithfully, you will choose to praise Him. You will sing above the sorrow. You will refuse to engage with the devil for at least a few minutes every day, taking every thought captive for Christ as your pen records His kindness. What good has He done? How did He show up? What beauty did He bear? For what can you give thanks?

It won't always be easy.

But do it. Every day. Let's see where it takes us.

Elizabeth Foss

TO PONDER WITH YOUR PEN

Flip to the back of the book. Find the gratitude journal we've created for your thanksgiving. Embellish it if you like. Make it yours and love it well.

THREE *day*

MATTHEW 6: 25-33 (NRSV-CE)

"Therefore I tell you, do not worry about your life, what you will eat or what you will drink, or about your body, what you will wear. Is not life more than food, and the body more than clothing? Look at the birds of the air; they neither sow nor reap nor gather into barns, and yet your heavenly Father feeds them. Are you not of more value than they? And can any of you by worrying add a single hour to your span of life? And why do you worry about clothing? Consider the lilies of the field, how they grow; they neither toil nor spin, yet I tell you, even Solomon in all his glory was not clothed like one of these. But if God so clothes the grass of the field, which is alive today and tomorrow is thrown into the oven, will he not much more clothe you—you of little faith? Therefore do not worry, saying, 'What will we eat?' or 'What will we drink?' or 'What will we wear?' For it is the Gentiles who strive for all these things; and indeed your heavenly Father knows that you need all these things. But strive first for the kingdom of God and his righteousness, and all these things will be given to you as well."

SONG OF SOLOMON 2:1-2 (NRSV-CE)

I am a rose of Sharon,
   a lily of the valleys.
As a lily among brambles,
   so is my love among maidens.

THINK UPON THESE THINGS

It was midsummer as I lay there, without hair, without white blood cells, without a way to escape what was happening in the bed next to me. I was the very young mother of a toddler son, fighting desperately to defeat cancer and reclaim the promise of a future. Just a few feet away, in the bed next to mine, the mother of two school-aged children was breaking the news to her loved ones that she would not live to see another summer. It was 1990. There were no iPhones, nor even iPods. My head screamed in pain as the opportunistic infection had its way, so the television tortured me instead of offering diversion and distraction. I couldn't hold a book to read. I was a prisoner of neutropenia and the chance proximity to the most sorrowful conversations I could have imagined.

A new friend came by, a woman with whom I'd been paired when I asked a cancer support network to please find me someone who'd survived my disease and my treatment, and (let's just shoot for the moon here) who'd gotten pregnant afterwards. She came bearing a Walkman and a mix tape of all of Amy Grant's songs. She knew. She knew that I needed songs of lament and of praise to minister to my frightened and sorrowful soul. I spent the next five days listening on endless repeat.

Amy Grant sang directly into my ear and she was the only thing I heard, effectively eliminating hospital noise and focusing my attention on God's provision. The song *Jehovah*, in particular, brought me peace. I listened to the words and took their message to heart. Her voice drew me into a peaceful pasture and asked me to ponder the lilies growing there. She assured me that He'd care for me just as He cared for them, but that I was even more precious to the Lord.

And so I did. Over and over again, I envisioned those lilies. In my mind, they were sweet, tender, white, and fragrant. Years later, I would stumble upon the Song of Solomon and recognize them there—the lily-of-the-valley among the brambles, His love song to His daughter. Tentatively at first, but with fervor later, I let myself believe that He would indeed look after each and every need. A cradle Catholic, I had a serious conversion experience in a hospital bed on 9 West, when I was twenty-four. Forever more, that song, in particular, was my anthem. Two years later, when our son was born, we named him Matthew, for the precious verses from the sixth chapter of Matthew that brought hope and healing to our darkest days.

Three times in these verses, our Lord tells us not to be anxious. I wish I could tell you that I conquered fear once and for all in the summer of 1990. I did not. My prayers for children were answered with astonishing generosity (I have nine). All these years later, I have learned that seven teenagers have meant countless opportunities to worry. Life constantly tempts me with anxiety.

The Lord is quite firm: worry is futile. It does not add anything of value to our lives. Worry doesn't prevent bad things from happening. It doesn't save us from the seemingly capricious acts of fate that rock our worlds. It doesn't make us wiser or more capable. It certainly doesn't make us holier.

Worry tempts us to play God. Like the pagans of Jesus' day—like those of little faith here and now—we who worry are tormented by the notion that we are at the mercy of a merciless fate. Nothing could be further from the truth. We are tenderly held in the capable hands of a benevolent God. What's more, He knows exactly what we need! He knows better than we do.

God asks us to exchange our anxiety for trusting obedience. He wants us to seek nothing but His kingdom and, if we do, He promises that all that we need will be added unto us. Every last need. So, I ask you to sing with me—songs of lament to be sure, but also songs of clear-eyed faith, the anthems of hope that ultimately triumph over fear and sorrow.

Elizabeth Foss

TO PONDER WITH YOUR PEN

Are you anxious? About what do you worry? Where is God in that worry? When do you call Him in? If you're inclined to draw, let today's prayer get you started.

LIFTED TO THE LORD

Dear Lord, my heart is troubled. I carry the cares of my world tightly knotted up inside my soul. Help me trust you to untangle the knots and to see how those ribbons can gather the lilies for me.

day FOUR

1 THESSALONIANS 5: 13-25 (NRSV-CE)

…Be at peace among yourselves. And we urge you, beloved, to admonish the idlers, encourage the fainthearted, help the weak, be patient with all of them. See that none of you repays evil for evil, but always seek to do good to one another and to all. Rejoice always, pray without ceasing, give thanks in all circumstances; for this is the will of God in Christ Jesus for you. Do not quench the Spirit. Do not despise the words of prophets, but test everything; hold fast to what is good; abstain from every form of evil.

May the God of peace himself sanctify you entirely; and may your spirit and soul and body be kept sound and blameless at the coming of our Lord Jesus Christ. The one who calls you is faithful, and he will do this.

Beloved, pray for us.

For further reading: Romans 12:12, Ephesians 4:1-16

THINK UPON THESE THINGS

For most of my life, my identity has been defined by my strength and competency. Then last year, an accumulation of burnout and post-traumatic stress from a life lived with too much giving (and not enough rest) morphed into an anxiety disorder that left me unable to perform the most basic daily duties. Often just the effort to get out of bed sent me to the bathroom nauseous and dizzy.

As difficult as it was to live with the foreignness of this anxiety and depression that had made me a stranger to myself, it was compounded by the fact that my understanding of God was also enveloped in a fog of confusion. What had long been a personal and intimate relationship with my Savior was suddenly clouded with questions and doubts. I questioned whether God could be who I thought He was if I was no longer who I thought He wanted me to be.

What I have learned as I sought healing, both medically and spiritually is that all these verses in the Word of God that I so often applied to others—encouraging the faint-hearted, healing the weak, being patient with all of them—also apply to the way we treat ourselves. Being at peace among yourselves can also mean seeking peace with yourself.

For it is a God of peace who sanctifies us and makes our bodies and spirits sound. I had thought that, as my mind and body became more and more unsound, I became less in God's eyes. And that thought led me to wonder if I was forced to trade strength for fragility and competency, and achievement for slowness and stillness, could God still be who He was before?

Could I believe that the One who calls me is faithful and He will do this? That He will bring value to this weakness that feels so confining to me? Can He really bring life from the death of all that I once valued in myself?

As I continue to work toward recovery, I am coming not only to believe in the truth of the faithfulness of my God and His desire to do this for me—this healing, this renewal, this learning to offer kindness and compassion to myself—but I am holding onto it as my very life. God is clearing the fog and showing me His unchanging heart, where His love for me is unmoved by my undoing.

God is my Father and I am His child, and He is teaching me to walk again. If I reach for His hand and trust His strength, my steps will steady. For He is my unchanging, faithful Father, and He will do this for me. Even when I am uncertain of who I am, I can be certain of who God is. I can encourage my fainthearted self, and seek healing in my weakness, and be patient with all of me, because I know that God is sanctifying me entirely in His unchanging love.

Colleen Mitchell

TO PONDER WITH YOUR PEN

You try to be patient with other people. You speak gently to children (or at least you set out to speak gently). You are open and accepting when a friend shares her struggles, offering nurturing encouragement. Can you be patient with yourself today? Can you speak words of encouragement into your own fainthearted insecurities? Do that. Be gentle and kind and good with your words, here on this page, and there in your head.

_____

_____

_____

_____

_____

_____

_____

_____

_____

_____

_____

_____

_____

_____

_____

_____

LIFTED TO THE LORD
Today, Lord, inspire in my heart only words of encouragement toward myself. Let me forgive myself for my failings, remembering that You forgive me and that I am not to hold myself to a standard that I have exalted over Yours.

day FIVE

ISAIAH 40:10-11 (NRSV-CE)

See, the Lord God comes with might,
   and his arm rules for him;
his reward is with him,
   and his recompense before him.
He will feed his flock like a shepherd;
   he will gather the lambs in his arms,
and carry them in his bosom,
   and gently lead the mother sheep.

Further reading: Psalm 23, John 10:11-18

THINK UPON THESE THINGS

After the birth of our first child, my husband and I drove away from the hospital with an empty car seat, and everything felt wrong. Our son was tucked in a tiny incubator in the NICU, and leaving the hospital without him, I felt as if a part of me was ripped away.

The following nights I lie awake, worrying that my baby felt abandoned, torturing myself imagining that he and I would never properly bond because of our early separation. The excitement and anticipation I'd felt when I was pregnant was replaced with anxiety and fear. And despite our son's improvement, the day when he might finally come home still seemed impossibly far away.

We took a small sense of comfort, however, in the religious tokens that appeared in his crib throughout his NICU stay. First, it was a holy card of his patron Saint. Next came a tiny plastic rosary. A few days later, there was a picture of Mary the Mother of God, and on and on it went. Despite not knowing where they came from, we were grateful for these small gifts and their reminder to turn to God in our fear.

Then, one afternoon when my husband was holding our son in the NICU, a nun came to visit. She gave my husband a prayer card, and promised that she'd come back later to hold our little boy for a few hours. She explained that she'd visited every day since his birth, and when we couldn't be there, she held our baby and comforted him in our absence.

When my husband told me what he'd discovered, I was overcome with gratitude. And while it was still painful to leave the NICU the following day, I felt a sense of peace I hadn't before. Not only did I trust that the nun would once again visit our son, but her example of tender love had opened my eyes to a deeper comfort: Although my son spent hours in the NICU without us, he was never really alone. For, just as the nun held him each day in her loving arms, so did Jesus.

In Scripture, Jesus explains the way He lovingly cares for us by calling Himself the Good Shepherd (John 10). He is the One who "will gather the lambs in his arms, and carry them in his bosom" (Isaiah 40). And as a shepherd knows each of his sheep, Jesus knows each of us personally and intimately. As a shepherd ensures the safety of his sheep by never leaving even one alone to fend for itself, Jesus is always by our side.

Just as we can trust in the Good Shepherd's love and care for us, we can also trust that when we are limited in our ability to care for and love others, Jesus is there to provide what we cannot. Like the kind nun who cared for my son in my absence, Jesus' presence fills what is left empty. And because His love is perfect, what He gives not only fills our cups, but causes them to overflow in abundance. Indeed, the Lord is our Shepherd, and with Him, there is nothing we should want (Psalm 23).

Allison McGinley

TO PONDER WITH YOUR PEN

When you read today's verses, how does the image of God as a shepherd awaken in you new ways of thinking about His presence in your life?

_____

_____

_____

_____

_____

_____

_____

_____

_____

_____

_____

_____

_____

_____

_____

_____

LIFTED TO THE LORD

Dear Jesus, thank you for tenderly keeping watch over me.
Thank you for all the times you've rescued me and carried me safely
back into the sheepfold.

day
SIX

MATTHEW 8:23-27 (NRSV-CE)

And when he got into the boat, his disciples followed him. A windstorm arose on the sea, so great that the boat was being swamped by the waves; but he was asleep. And they went and woke him up, saying, "Lord, save us! We are perishing!" And he said to them, "Why are you afraid, you of little faith?" Then he got up and rebuked the winds and the sea; and there was a dead calm. They were amazed, saying, "What sort of man is this, that even the winds and the sea obey him?"

THINK UPON THESE THINGS

My Dad was an epic storyteller. I didn't appreciate his talent in my youth. I'd roll my eyes and suffer through the retelling of one sea story after another, promising myself never to inflict such pain upon my own children. However, there was one story I've held close to my heart since I first heard it in adolescence.

My father served in the US Navy during the Vietnam War. As a young naval officer, he stood night watch as officer of the deck aboard the destroyer USS Higbee. He told us stories about the sudden storms that appeared in the Tonkin Gulf. The sun would be shining brightly one moment, then, suddenly, the clouds would gather and block the light. Then the rain pelted sideways and the wind tossed the big ship about. Sailors would get instantly seasick from the rough waves.

Dad described how helpless they all felt being at the beck and call of nature; "We had to be always prepared for the worst. Our men were counting on us to be there to support them; it didn't matter if there was a storm or not. I've never prayed harder in my life than during those storms. I learned that trusting God with my safety, and that of my men, was the only way to survive the war. I relied on His provision in every situation. He never left my side then, and He remains vigilant even today."

Trust in the Lord...

Dad impressed upon us that storms come and go, but if we remained calm and kept our eyes on the Lord, the storm would pass and the lesson needing to be learned would remain, preparing us for the next storm. He described the sunshine and peace right behind the chaos of a bad storm. "If you looked to the sky," he would say, "you could almost see God's hand pushing the clouds away, bringing brilliant sunlight and calm, peaceful seas. Almost always, a rainbow would break out and everyone would take a deep breath, knowing the worst had passed. The same can be said for life. Remain calm, believe in the Lord's dominion over all and His provision for you, and all will be well."

In today's reading, the apostles are freaked out by a stormy sea. They panic. They don't know what to do. Jesus is sound asleep, and when they cannot take one more second of being tossed about like popcorn, they wake Him up, begging and pleading for His help. He responds, "Why are you afraid, you of little faith?" Jesus then moves to calm the seas, showing His dominion over them. The apostles look on in astonishment.

Isn't it the same for us? Storms in life come and go. We suffer spiritual attacks every day, sometimes all day, and we grow weary and are unsure of God's dominion over our lives. We panic. We cry out, begging Him to save us amid the difficulty, revealing to Him our lack of trust in His plan for our lives. Yet God—an ever loving, merciful, and kind God—pushes those clouds of darkness away, proclaiming His love in the brilliant sunlight. The seas are calmed and the rainbow of hope appears once more in the sky. The lesson learned is the same every single time. The goal is to remember it *before* and *during* the storm, not just after.

Trust in the Lord, for He is good and His mercy and grace will sustain you.

It's not just a saying. It's a promise.

Mary Lenaburg

TO PONDER WITH YOUR PEN

We share faith in our stories. What stories of God's faithfulness are ones that you will leave as a legacy?

_____

_____

_____

_____

_____

_____

_____

_____

_____

_____

_____

_____

_____

_____

_____

_____

_____

_____

_____

LIFTED TO THE LORD

I see you, God, standing in the bow of the boat, strong and sure, the Master of the sea and the Master of my life. Calm my storms.

day SEVEN

HIDE IT IN YOUR HEART

Today is a day to rest and be grateful. Take some time to look over your journaling from the week, to read a little more, to catch up on days when you didn't have as much time as you would have liked.

Spend a few moments looking carefully at our memory verse, to burn the image into your brain. These verses were chosen to give you the words of God, hidden in your heart, to use to talk back to the negative voices that might echo in your head. They were also chosen to give women words with which to minister to one another. These are the foundation of a common language of tenderness and compassion. When we are met with one another's misery, we won't have to fumble to find the words; we'll have God's Word. One more thing: if there is a child in your life, teach these words to him or her. They will serve that child for a lifetime. Don't be surprised when the child memorizes more easily than you do, even when the verses are longer. This memory work is a gift, a legacy. Hiding the Word of God in the heart of child is stocking her soul with saving grace. Together, take on this joyful endeavor. We're right there with you.

Practice writing the verse here.

MATTHEW 6:28- 29

…Consider the lilies of the field, how they grow; they neither toil nor spin, yet I tell you, even Solomon in all his glory was not clothed like one of these.

consider the lilies
OF THE FIELD, HOW THEY
grow
they neither toil
nor spin
YET I TELL YOU, EVEN SOLOMON IN
all his glory
WAS NOT CLOTHED LIKE
one of these

MATTHEW 6:28- 29

EIGHT *day*

PSALM 7:1-5 (NRSV-CE)

O Lord my God, in you I take refuge;
  save me from all my pursuers, and deliver me,

or like a lion they will tear me apart;
  they will drag me away, with no one to rescue.

O Lord my God, if I have done this,
  if there is wrong in my hands,

if I have repaid my ally with harm
  or plundered my foe without cause,

then let the enemy pursue and overtake me,
  trample my life to the ground,
  and lay my soul in the dust. Selah

For further reading: Read all of Psalm 71 to see how our Lord teaches us to lament.

THINK UPON THESE THINGS

I remember how her mother told me that if she didn't come downstairs smiling every morning, she was sharply spanked and sent back upstairs to try again. There would be no crying, no protest, no other way to start the day except for cheerfulness. A good Christian, said the mother, is always cheerful. She was six years old. That story has stuck with me for thirty years.

About a third of the psalms are psalms of lament. God gives us the poetry and the pattern to make our own prayer when we want to cry out. Lament is honest. It is the cry of the soul that is still faithful, even in pain. It is the honest seeking for answers while trusting in the One who has them. It is plaintive prayer that we do believe will be answered.

The good Father doesn't send us back upstairs with a spanking when our hearts are troubled and our countenance reflects a sad soul. Instead, He allows us to acknowledge that each of us lives in an afflicted body, moving about in a world scarred by sin. He invites us to take up the sorrowful song of the psalmist. God knows that when affliction envelops us, we change. We break. Once broken, we are not put back together in exactly the same way. We are transformed into something new. The prayer of lament is the pathway to transformation. Prayer doesn't change God's mind. Prayer changes us.

The psalmist shows us how to lament, how to pray. He asks for God's attention, and then complains that he is in the grasp of the wicked. He reminds the Lord (and in doing so, reminds himself) that he has trusted Him since he was a child, and then he begs again for God's intervention. Tucked in the middle is one of my favorite exhortations. We hear it daily in the Liturgy of the Hours: Lord, make haste to help me! I sprinkle that one liberally throughout my day. Finally, the psalmist preaches to himself. He speaks words of assurance into his own soul; he promises that he will praise God no matter how his prayers are answered. Even in the struggle, he will continue to hope and he will continue to praise.

Lament brings before God all the muck that clouds our souls. It's honest. It's not sugar-coated cheerfulness with bile beneath the candy shell. It's all the agony prayed through tears of hope and trust. We take to Him our anger, our pain, our sorrow, our deepest fears. All of it wells up and out of ourselves to be laid at the foot of His cross. There, it sits in the full light of His truth. There, He is able to begin the work of healing the brokenness in our souls.

Elizabeth Foss

TO PONDER WITH YOUR PEN

Pen your own psalm of lament. Sometimes, we must pray the words and then wait in hope for our hearts to catch up. Begin by praising the Lord and telling Him of the times you've trusted and He's been faithful. Then, pour out your pain, your fears, your disappointments. Conclude by reassuring your soul that God is your hope and you are forever His.

_____

_____

_____

_____

_____

_____

_____

_____

_____

_____

_____

_____

_____

_____

_____

_____

_____

_____

_____

LIFTED TO THE LORD

Today, at every suffering, large or small, beg the prayer, "Lord, make haste to help me!" Let it become your new habit.

day NINE

PSALM 42:1-2 (NRSV-CE)

As a deer longs for flowing streams,
  so my soul longs for you, O God.
My soul thirsts for God,
  for the living God.
When shall I come and behold
  the face of God?

For further reading: read all of Psalm 42 to see the language of the psalmist as he seeks the face of God.

THINK UPON THESE THINGS

I am one of those people who wanders the racks at Target having a conversation with herself. Sometimes—more times than I'd like to admit—you might even hear me talking out loud. For me, shopping is stressful. I'm overwhelmed by choices. I'm annoyed that nothing fits me like it does the mannequins. I'm limited by my budget, but not by my imagination. And so I mutter. Sometimes, I coach myself into a better place. Most times, I'm sad to admit, I just keep listening to my own nonsense. And there's the fine distinction: is your interior dialogue helpful or is it your own worst enemy because it knows your misery buttons better than anyone else? Do you coach yourself, using the grammar of hope, or do you listen to yourself, repeating the lies that batter your soul?

The psalmist is discouraged. God lets us see the interior dialogue of discouragement and His Word offers us very specific insight about how to respond. Like me (and you?), in the face of trouble, he asks God *why*? Whenever I reach out to someone who is newly diagnosed with cancer, I tell her to beware the night. It's in the nighttime, when the world is still and dark, that fear and desolation comes rushing in and the battle within your own mind for peace is fierce. The psalmist is clearly well acquainted with this phenomenon. His strategy is to "sing the night." It's not a song of praise, but of pleading. He is singing for his life! He's desperate, but he's determined.

Even though he assures himself that God is with him, he also expresses the sense that God has forgotten him. Those words of abandonment are words that he utters to give them release, not words of conviction. He feels forgotten, despite the intellectual understanding that he is never forgotten. Clearly, there's a place to tell God we feel like He's left us, even when we know that it's not true.

Throughout his lament, the psalmist keeps coming back to the reality that God loves him. He keeps reassuring himself that even though his soul is riding on the crest of waves and crashing about inside him like thunder, God is in control. Even the storms that rage inside him are held within the capable hands of the Creator who loves him. He remembers God's faithfulness. You too, can remember. That gratitude list you are keeping will help you remember specific instances of His goodness. The psalmist isn't soft-pedaling his pain. He acknowledges the intensity of his feelings. And then, instead of listening to his own wailing, he intersperses repeated reassurances that he is loved and held. The "waves and billows" of life can be formidable; still, God is the ruler of wind and wave. He's got this. Can we do that? Can we acknowledge our despair, but then speak words of God's wisdom and love into that despair?

We can and we must. We need to preach to our souls. We need to coach ourselves. Like the psalmist, we can speak the very words of hope into the part of us that knows God. More progressive translations drop the words "O, my soul" from the fifth verse. That's too bad. Here, the psalmist gives us the great gift of knowing that we can speak directly into our souls. *Why am I depressed? Why the turmoil, Soul of mine? Put your hope in God, Soul. (v. 11)* Those are the words of hope. Hope is the water parched souls desperately need. Speak them **to your soul.**

But which words of hope will you speak? This psalmist did not know Christ. We do. The gospel is our hope. The work that lies before the person who is weary and woeful is the "work" of learning and knowing the unchanging Word of God. When we know the gospel, we know God and we know who we are in God. We are calmed and cheered by the deep down understanding of what He did and what He is going to do. We thirst for the intimate knowledge of Him. That knowledge brings peace. We can find the actual language of hope between the covers of our Bibles. The time you invest in the Word in the morning is given back to you when the middle of the night darkness begins to envelop you. Speak the morning hope to it. Then, like the psalmist, you are able to genuinely praise Him because you've given drink to your thirsty soul with the living water of the Word.

Elizabeth Foss

TO PONDER WITH YOUR PEN

Here is the space to use to seek the face of God. Call out to Him and ask Him to meet you in the cares of this day.

_____

_____

_____

_____

_____

_____

_____

_____

_____

_____

_____

_____

_____

_____

_____

_____

_____

_____

LIFTED TO THE LORD

Thank you, God, for the language of hope. Thank you being the good Author of my story of triumph.

day TEN

JOB 13:13-1 (NRSV-CE)

Let me have silence, and I will speak,
  and let come on me what may.
I will take my flesh in my teeth,
  and put my life in my hand.
See, he will kill me; I have no hope;
  but I will defend my ways to his face.
This will be my salvation,
  that the godless shall not come before him.

2 CORINTHIANS 1:3-11 (NRSV-CE)

Blessed be the God and Father of our Lord Jesus Christ, the Father of mercies and the God of all consolation, who consoles us in all our affliction, so that we may be able to console those who are in any affliction with the consolation with which we ourselves are consoled by God. For just as the sufferings of Christ are abundant for us, so also our consolation is abundant through Christ. If we are being afflicted, it is for your consolation and salvation; if we are being consoled, it is for your consolation, which you experience when you patiently endure the same sufferings that we are also suffering. Our hope for you is unshaken; for we know that as you share in our sufferings, so also you share in our consolation.
We do not want you to be unaware, brothers and sisters, of the affliction we experienced in Asia; for we were so utterly, unbearably crushed that we despaired of life itself. Indeed, we felt that we had received the sentence of death so that we would rely not on ourselves but on God who raises the dead. He who rescued us from so deadly a peril will continue to rescue us; on him we have set our hope that he will rescue us again, as you also join in helping us by your prayers, so that many will give thanks on our behalf for the blessing granted us through the prayers of many.

For further reading: Job 2, Romans 8:18-28

THINK UPON THESE THINGS

Her voice was thick with hurt and disappointment when she called. "Please come pick me up, and please, on the drive home, can we just not talk about it?" I had my orders. I gave her a hug, watched her get settled into the seat beside me, and drove in silence for the first half hour. Then, the words came. Slowly at first, and then a torrent with tears. Still I was mostly silent. In the days to come, I was invited to console, and asked to advise, but on the long car ride home, my only role was keep watch over the lament.

There is a time for tears, a time for lament, a time to sob in sorrow. We have seen David cry out to God, pouring his complaints out to the Lord, begging for consolation and asking why God has forsaken him. Now we consider Job. We know Job as the icon of suffering. He is covered with sores all over his body. He's felt the absolute greatest grief of a parent burying his child; he's felt it ten times! The wife who has built a life with him, stood by him as everything was lost, and nursed him in his agony has suggested that maybe he'd be better off dead—even his dearest companion doesn't sound like herself. Everyone and everything is lost.

He remains faithful. He feels like there is no hope--that God will allow him to die. The footnote for verse 15 reads *"Though he kill me, yet I will trust in him."* Even unto death, Job trusts. Like David, he is steadfast. He clearly expresses that he doesn't like what is happening, but he just as clearly expresses his faith. Both Job and David wail before their King, praying their feelings out loud. And God meets them in their groanings.

Job's friends sit with him for seven days and say not a word. There is a time for sitting with someone in the silence. Too often, we rush in and our words—even scriptural words—fall flat and sound stiff because it's not yet time for them to be received.

Maybe we should let the grief and the sorrow and the bitterness run freely from eyes that grow swollen and ugly. Witnesses to pain must pray for patience. When the time does come to comfort, can we take our cues from Saint Paul? Far from reserved, he hits friends over the head with consolation, repeating the word five times in one sentence and four in the next. The editor in me twitches at the redundancy. I want to ask him to vary his word choice. But it's the inspired Word of God, so I refrain, pause, ponder. And pray. Why say it so insistently? Does God know I won't hear it the first, or even the third time?

Saint Paul wants to share the good news that after the lament, after coming to a place where we are so utterly, unbearably crushed that we are despaired of life itself, God saves.

The hope Saint Paul had was in Jesus Christ who rose from the dead. That same God wanted to hear Saint Paul's lament. He wanted to hear Job's lament and David's lament. He wants to hear your lament. Suffering gets our attention and then, we can turn that attention to God in our lament.

He hears you and He moves towards the sound of your voice. There will come a time when you look back to a season of lament and see how God was working to bring everything together for good. You will see the transformative role lament had in that season. There will be a time, when, like Paul, you can tell what a wondrous thing God has done for you, how He brought you back from the brink of death. You will say again and again that God is the Great Consoler. For now, though, just know that God hears you in your sadness, and He listens intently to your worry. He wants to sit with you in the pain.

Elizabeth Foss

TO PONDER WITH YOUR PEN

If you are in a season of lament, can you remember a time when you were more at peace? Describe that time. Where was God in that? Were you acutely aware of Him then? Are you more aware now, or less? What does your understanding of lament tell you about the nature of God? How does it affect your relationship with Him?

_____

_____

_____

_____

_____

_____

_____

_____

_____

_____

_____

_____

_____

_____

_____

_____

LIFTED TO THE LORD

Dear Lord, my heart is troubled. I carry the cares of my world tightly knotted up inside my soul. Help me trust you to untangle the knots and to see how those ribbons can gather the lilies for me.

day ELEVEN

PROVERBS 12:25 (NRSV-CE)

Anxiety weighs down the human heart,
  but a good word cheers it up.

PROVERBS 15:4 (NRSV-CE)

A gentle tongue is a tree of life,
  but perverseness in it breaks the spirit.

THINK UPON THESE THINGS

Late one evening, I was completely overwhelmed. My husband was traveling for several days, and at least one of our kids found their way into our bed each night he was gone. Long days of activities punctuated by numerous traffic jams had exhausted us, and now the youngest was sick. After trying to console her for three hours, my thoughts turned ugly and self-deprecating. *You can't do this,* I told myself. *You're not enough.* Then of course, the guilt followed. *You're a terrible mother,* I thought. *How can you be so frustrated with an innocent child?*

I remembered the pain of not knowing whether I'd be able to have more children after multiple rounds of chemotherapy, and that skyrocketed my guilt to new heights. Once my mind returned to the cancer that rocked our lives, I couldn't stop the familiar anxiety that still plagued me, fueled by my fear of a recurrence and worse, the thought of one of my children someday being afflicted by such a serious illness. I began crying as my little girl wailed in my arms, and the night ahead appeared endless and my weaknesses countless.

But I'd teetered on the edge of despair before, and knew the consuming darkness that overcomes us when we believe Satan's lies and resign ourselves to defeat. So, I grabbed my phone and texted my five closest friends, asking for their prayers. I shut out the voice in my head that whispered how self-centered I was acting when so many others were undoubtedly going through much worse. I simply asked for prayers—no qualifying words or apology offered.

As my phone buzzed with messages of encouragement and promises of prayers, I began to breathe easier and felt more at peace. A wise friend included a verse from Scripture reminding me that weeping might last through the night, but joy would come in the morning (Psalm 30:5). Buoyed by comforting words from faithful friends and the Word of God, I was able to emerge from my self-indulgence and offer my daughter the love and comfort she needed and deserved. The night remained difficult and long, but sustained by the grace of God and the prayers of those who loved me, I made it through.

When the walls seem to be closing in, it's tempting to slam the door shut, curl into a ball, and burrow further into the darkness. But alone in the dark, we stumble over our own feet and flail blindly with our hands, searching for the door. If, instead, we summon the courage and humility to ask friends or family for help, and look to the Word of God for comfort and wisdom, we leave the door ajar, just enough to let the light shine in.

Allison McGinley

TO PONDER WITH YOUR PEN

Who are the people you can call or text when you need encouragement and support? Who can you count on to remind you of God's help and to intercede on your behalf? Make a list of them here, and also jot a note to yourself about how they've been there for you. Remember to reach out and thank them for their faithfulness in prayer.

_____

_____

_____

_____

_____

_____

_____

_____

_____

_____

_____

_____

_____

_____

_____

_____

_____

LIFTED TO THE LORD

Dear Jesus, thank you for the gift of friends who answer phone calls and texts with promises to pray. I'm grateful for their support and for the strength they implore from You on my behalf. Please open my heart to the prayer concerns of the people around me. Let me be a trusted intercessor for them.

TWELVE day

EPHESIANS 6:10-18 (NRSV-CE)

Finally, be strong in the Lord and in the strength of his power. Put on the whole armor of God, so that you may be able to stand against the wiles of the devil. For our struggle is not against enemies of blood and flesh, but against the rulers, against the authorities, against the cosmic powers of this present darkness, against the spiritual forces of evil in the heavenly places. Therefore take up the whole armor of God, so that you may be able to withstand on that evil day, and having done everything, to stand firm. Stand therefore, and fasten the belt of truth around your waist, and put on the breastplate of righteousness. As shoes for your feet put on whatever will make you ready to proclaim the gospel of peace. With all of these, take the shield of faith, with which you will be able to quench all the flaming arrows of the evil one. Take the helmet of salvation, and the sword of the Spirit, which is the word of God.

Pray in the Spirit at all times in every prayer and supplication. To that end keep alert and always persevere in supplication for all the saints.

For further reading: Hebrews 1:14, Matthew 18: 10, 2 Corinthians 10:3-5

THINK UPON THESE THINGS

I was recently diagnosed with an autoimmune disease, and, in the weeks since, I have spent hours researching the best ways to manage this disease and encourage healing. A recurring theme in my reading has been the importance of stress management. Unfortunately, I am wildly deficient in that department. I don't manage stress; I collect and compound it. Some days, my never-ending to-do list threatens to swallow me whole.

Having recognized poor stress management as one of my weaknesses, I also understand that this is a place where I have long been weathering spiritual attack. Satan loves to strike where we are weakest, and he's got me pegged. There is certainly a battle being waged here. As I formulate a plan for moving forward, I must look beyond the obvious basics of self-care. The enemy's goal is to steal my hope. He wants to convince me that there is truly no rest for the weary.

Recognizing that this is undoubtedly a battle, I know I need a solid plan if I'm going to survive. I need tactics. To start, I must take captive those thoughts that signal the beginning of a downward spiral—the *I'll never get it all done and I'm failing at this* thoughts. Because there is rest in Jesus; this is the truth of our faith. My ultimate goal is not to complete all the tasks that lie ahead of me. There's no lasting satisfaction in a checked-off list, because tomorrow will bring another. The calming of my mind will only come from marking my days for Him and with Him.

To do so, I must add intention to my days and be firm in my resolve. Each day should begin not only with prayer, but with Scripture as well. The Bible tells us to put on the whole armor of God, the greatest weapon of which is the sword of the Spirit, the Word of God.

Keeping a Bible next to my bed will help remind me when I wake to pick it up, to read, to pray. A second Bible, on my work table in our living area, can easily be picked up when I sit down to nurse the baby. A midday break, perhaps offers time for a few verses and more prayer. These moments, though brief, can serve to mark my day for Christ, reminding me that my time is His. At the end of the day, I find time for a few more verses, and always my final prayers before going to sleep. Only time spent in the Word, and in prayer, will help quiet the constant go, go, go, and give me the rest I truly need.

Ginny Sheller

TO PONDER WITH YOUR PEN

Make your to-do list. Go ahead: list every last thing you want to accomplish today. Try to list the items in the order you will do them. Now, using a different color pen, write in all the times you will stop and listen to the Lord of your time in His Word. See where you have room for Him in your day.

_____

_____

_____

_____

_____

_____

_____

_____

_____

_____

_____

_____

_____

_____

_____

_____

_____

_____

LIFTED TO THE LORD

Sweet Jesus, when I am still and quiet, I know that You are the master of time. As soon as I start to move through my day, I lose sight of that truth. Please remind me today to take a few moments throughout my day to reconnect with You in Scripture.

day THIRTEEN

JEREMIAH 29:11-14 (NRSV-CE)

For surely I know the plans I have for you, says the Lord, plans for your welfare and not for harm, to give you a future with hope. Then when you call upon me and come and pray to me, I will hear you. When you search for me, you will find me; if you seek me with all your heart, I will let you find me, says the Lord, and I will restore your fortunes and gather you from all the nations and all the places where I have driven you, says the Lord, and I will bring you back to the place from which I sent you into exile.

ROMANS 5:1-5 (NRSV-CE)

Therefore, since we are justified by faith, we have peace with God through our Lord Jesus Christ, through whom we have obtained access to this grace in which we stand; and we boast in our hope of sharing the glory of God. And not only that, but we also boast in our sufferings, knowing that suffering produces endurance, and endurance produces character, and character produces hope, and hope does not disappoint us, because God's love has been poured into our hearts through the Holy Spirit that has been given to us.

THINK UPON THESE THINGS

"Want to know a lot about your family and friends? Get cancer." Junot Diaz, author of *The Brief Wondrous Life of Oscar Wao*, visited my university and said this line while discussing personal apocalypses and what they reveal. Saint Paul asks us to take on a herculean task: to boast in our sufferings with the knowledge that suffering produces hope. He seems to present a simple sequence for doing so, but it's deceptively challenging. Let's break that down, step by step.

First, boasting. In one of my favorite homilies as a child, our priest discussed what it meant to bring our Catholic faith into the world. He explained that it meant saying grace as a family at a restaurant, but it did not mean rising, clinking your glass, and announcing "Everyone! I am about to say grace! In the name of the Father..." Saint Paul is expecting something similar for us here. This boast is not a boast to fellow man, but to God himself. He's asking us to be proud of sufferings that will bring us closer to Christ, helping us to achieve our goal of meeting our Father in paradise.

This does not sound fun. Boasting in my sufferings is not my favorite call to action. But Saint Paul reminds us that suffering produces endurance. All who have run a marathon or suffered through tragedy or trauma know that endurance is nothing to sneeze at. In fact, to endure–to engage in a heroic stand, while remaining patient—is heralded by Milton in *Paradise Lost* as the ultimate Christ-like action. When Jesus is tempted in the desert, He does not retaliate by blasting Satan into oblivion with legions of angels. He simply *stands*. He simply endures. This is far from easy. This is *heroic*. This endurance, this perseverance, is a true act of love.

It makes sense, then, that this loving endurance produces character. That means— and this is a rather unnerving thought, but it is true—we become our personal apocalypses. How we endure will reveal a great deal about the kind of people we truly are. Here, for me, is Saint Paul's biggest jump: that character produces hope. How does that work? How am I hopeful after all this suffering? God is tapping my shoulder, reminding me that we do not have to do this alone: "*For surely I know the plans I have for you.*" As Saint Paul says, when we stand with Christ, we stand in grace. We have hope and faith in Him.

Do you feel ashamed of how you have endured sometimes? Me too. It's human. That's what the gracious, life-giving sacraments are for—to start again, to fill us when we are empty. Our crosses will become our character; let's carry them beautifully. And don't forget to boast, to give yourself a pat on the back every once in a while when you stand tall, with grace, under the heaviness. This endurance is the heroic work of a lifetime, and it is rarely celebrated in this realm. Jesus and all the saints in heaven are watching you carry this weight and they know its burden, and they are seeing the character it produces. They are cheering for you. Make them proud.

Katy Greiner

TO PONDER WITH YOUR PEN

Junot Diaz's recipe for surviving personal apocalypses had the following ingredients:

Community   Struggle
Resilience   Creativity

Consider those ingredients in light of the crosses God asks you to carry. Ask Him to show you His plan for each in your life.

_____

_____

_____

_____

_____

_____

_____

_____

_____

_____

_____

_____

_____

_____

_____

_____

_____

LIFTED TO THE LORD

Dear Lord, when I am bowed under the weight of my burdens, it is easy to lose sight of the privilege it is to carry Your cross. It is also easy to lose sight of the fact that You carry it with me, and, that by the ministry of the Church, you offer to me the sacraments to strengthen me on my journey. Call me back to You, Lord. Keep me close. Make me a hero for You.

day FOURTEEN

HIDE IT IN YOUR HEART

Today is a day to rest and be grateful. Take some time to look over your journaling from the week, to read a little more, to catch up on days when you didn't have as much time as you would have liked. Practice writing the memory verse here, and make it your own on the facing page.

PHILIPPIANS 4:7 (NRSV-CE)

And the peace of God, which surpasses all understanding, will guard your hearts and your minds in Christ Jesus.

_____

_____

_____

_____

_____

_____

_____

_____

_____

_____

_____

_____

_____

_____

And the peace of God,
which surpasses all understanding,
will guard your hearts
and your minds in
Christ Jesus

FIFTEEN *day*

PSALM 73:21-28 (NRSV-CE)

When my soul was embittered,
  when I was pricked in heart,

I was stupid and ignorant;
  I was like a brute beast toward you.

Nevertheless I am continually with you;
  you hold my right hand.

You guide me with your counsel,
  and afterward you will receive me with honor.

Whom have I in heaven but you?
  And there is nothing on earth that I desire other than you.

My flesh and my heart may fail,
  but God is the strength of my heart and my portion forever.

Indeed, those who are far from you will perish;
  you put an end to those who are false to you.

But for me it is good to be near God;
  I have made the Lord God my refuge,
  to tell of all your works.

1 KINGS 5:4 (NRSV-CE)

But now the Lord my God has given me rest on every side; there is neither adversary nor misfortune.

1 CORINTHIANS 1:27 (NRSV-CE)

But God chose what is foolish in the world to shame the wise; God chose what is weak in the world to shame the strong;

MATTHEW 19:26 (NRSV-CE)

But Jesus looked at them and said, "For mortals it is impossible, but for God all things are possible."

For further reading: See the NIV translations of these: Jonah 2:6, Genesis 50:20

THINK UPON THESE THINGS

The first few lines of today's first verses capture the bitter heart of someone who is wounded to the core; he's so desolate that he pushes God away. In that moment, he is "stupid and ignorant" and he keeps repeating the same sad lies in his head, failing to recognize that the truth will set him free from the bondage of desperate hopelessness. And then, there is a blessed moment of clarity: *but God.*

Someone once told me that a popular television psychologist has made it known that, in relationships, nothing after "but" counts. The idea is that if you apologize or empathize, and then you say "but," you've negated what you said just before the "but."

I told my friend that it's a good thing that in our family, we read and speak according to the grammar of Good News, so we are not bound by Dr. TV's dubious pronouncements. We believe that what comes after the "but" is the best. Actually, we are a people who can—and should—answer the toxic lies we tell ourselves with "but God…"

Life happens. Hurt happens. Discouragement happens. We lose. We grieve.

And then we have a choice.

We can believe the "but God" clause, or we can drown in our despondency. No matter where the despair originates, it's a lack of faith that allows us to sink without so much as reaching for a flotation device. It's unbelief that makes no effort to resist the enveloping doom.

The psalmist writes that his body is broken and his heart is failing, but ultimately, his faith will not allow him to yield to destruction. He chooses to draw his strength from his Lord forever. He chooses to believe in the "but God."

When life seems too hard and we begin to spiral inward on ourselves, the sound of our voices inside our heads rings hollow and haunting.

I am not enough.
I am failing.
I am hurting.
I am rejected.
I am lonely.

We tell ourselves things about ourselves that we'd never utter to another human being. The internal dialogue is brutal. We are relentless purveyors of ugliness to ourselves. Maybe we think it's all true.

What happens when we follow every defeating statement with "…but God…"? I am not enough, *but God's power is made perfect in my weakness.* (See 2 Corinthians 12:9)

I am failing, *but God tells me to run with perseverance the race marked out for me.* (See Hebrews 12:1)

I am hurting, *but God promises He will wipe away every tear from my eyes, and death shall be no more, neither shall there be mourning, nor crying, nor pain, for the former things have passed away.* (See Revelation 21:4)

I am rejected, *but God knows that Jesus Himself was a living stone rejected by men but chosen and precious in the sight of God* (See 1 Peter 2:4)

I am lonely, *but God promises that He is with me. He tells me not to be dismayed because He will strengthen me, and help me, and hold me up with His own hand.* (See Isaiah 41:10)

It's the *but* that gives us hope. It's the *but* that gets us out of bed in the morning.

It's the *but* that rises victorious over despair.

Elizabeth Foss

TO PONDER WITH YOUR PEN

First, return to the verses for today in this journal. Highlight the words "but" and "God" in each verse. Then, find the verses in your Bible and underline them. Use these verses to talk back to yourself. Are you one whose interior dialogue is negative in ways that you'd never speak to anyone else? Put those negative words to paper and, at the end of every "statement," pen the words *but God* followed by what you know to be true and good about God and you.

_____

_____

_____

_____

_____

_____

_____

_____

_____

_____

_____

_____

_____

_____

_____

_____

LIFTED TO THE LORD

Lord, I believe that every message of defeat I say to myself was whispered to me first by the enemy. I believe that you came to overcome despair. Please remind me those messages of loss are just the first phrase. *But God* is the finisher that makes the statements true

SIXTEEN *day*

1 PETER 1:3-9 (NRSV-CE)

Blessed be the God and Father of our Lord Jesus Christ! By his great mercy he has given us a new birth into a living hope through the resurrection of Jesus Christ from the dead, and into an inheritance that is imperishable, undefiled, and unfading, kept in heaven for you, who are being protected by the power of God through faith for a salvation ready to be revealed in the last time. In this you rejoice, even if now for a little while you have had to suffer various trials, so that the genuineness of your faith—being more precious than gold that, though perishable, is tested by fire—may be found to result in praise and glory and honor when Jesus Christ is revealed. Although you have not seen him, you love him; and even though you do not see him now, you believe in him and rejoice with an indescribable and glorious joy, for you are receiving the outcome of your faith, the salvation of your souls.

THINK UPON THESE THINGS

Sleep has been a problem for me for much of my life, especially over the past sixteen years, during which I have had small children waking me frequently at night. This wouldn't be so terrible if I could fall back to sleep quickly after getting them settled. My husband has always possessed that gift, the ability to fall asleep in mere seconds, whether at bedtime, or after being awakened by a crying child. Not me.

Lately, I do manage to fall asleep a short time after going to bed, but after my baby daughter wakes me in the night to nurse, I struggle to fall back to sleep. My mind quickly travels to a place full of endless to-dos and worries. And then, thinking of how much I need to be sleeping, I become even more anxious, which pushes rest further away. It's truly a vicious cycle. I've tried many things to help myself over the years: repetitive prayers, essential oils, sometimes giving up and getting out of bed to knit for a while. In my prayers, I ask God to quiet my mind, and to help me go back to sleep, I find myself begging Him, *You know how much I need rest. Please, help!* Those sleepless times in the middle of the night tend to make me feel especially alone, abandoned even, particularly when my cries for peace seem to go unanswered.

On a recent night, after lying awake for what seemed like hours, heavy worries on my heart, it occurred to me that I might be going about this all wrong. Rather than begging for rest, I need instead to accept the trial of insomnia. Maybe this bit of suffering, exaggerated as it is by the darkness, could be used for my own good. Could it possibly even be a test of faith? Can I believe that God loves me, even when it seems that my prayers for sleep aren't answered in the way that I hope? Can I trust that God is using this time for my good? Perhaps the acceptance of both my tiredness and my wakefulness is the first step to overcoming my tendency to worry.

Rather than begging God to take this nighttime affliction, maybe I should ask Him to use insomnia to bring me closer to Jesus. According to my faith I know that truly I am never alone. Even on the loneliest of nights, I know Jesus is there. He is always with us in our darkest moments. By turning my thoughts to Him during my times of wide-awake worry, sleepless nights might serve as a gentle fire of refinement to help me surrender, accept this cross, and in doing so, draw closer to Him.

Ginny Sheller

TO PONDER WITH YOUR PEN

What are your strategies for rest? How do you plan for a good night's sleep? How can you plan now for your next sleepless night? Could you put a rosary beside your bed? Are there verses that have spoken to you throughout this study that you could write here, to memorize, so that you can pray God's Word in the dark? In the light of day, begin to plan how you will surrender in the dark.

_____

_____

_____

_____

_____

_____

_____

_____

_____

_____

_____

_____

_____

_____

_____

_____

LIFTED TO THE LORD

Before it even begins, I offer to You my next sleepless night. Remind me of this devotional time with You. When the nighttime threatens to envelop me in worry, hurry to my side and console me with Your Presence. In Jesus' name. Amen.

day SEVENTEEN

2 CORINTHIANS 12: 6-10 (NRSV-CE)

But if I wish to boast, I will not be a fool, for I will be speaking the truth. But I refrain from it, so that no one may think better of me than what is seen in me or heard from me, even considering the exceptional character of the revelations. Therefore, to keep me from being too elated, a thorn was given me in the flesh, a messenger of Satan to torment me, to keep me from being too elated. Three times I appealed to the Lord about this, that it would leave me, but he said to me, "My grace is sufficient for you, for power is made perfect in weakness." So, I will boast all the more gladly of my weaknesses, so that the power of Christ may dwell in me. Therefore I am content with weaknesses, insults, hardships, persecutions, and calamities for the sake of Christ; for whenever I am weak, then I am strong.

THINK UPON THESE THINGS

Just last weekend at a women's retreat, a friend pointed out that this reading says power is made perfect in weakness. Our weakness is not simply tolerated by God and made acceptable by His strength, but our weakness is an opportunity for His power to be made perfect.

I don't much like being weak. Fragility—whether mental, emotional, or physical—has been something to be avoided at all costs in my life. The cost of that avoidance recently has been a breaking that has made me more fragile than I ever could have imagined myself. I carry this fragility like Paul did the thorn in his flesh. I beg the Lord to take it away. And He keeps returning with the same answer: *Will you be fragile for me, so that I can use this weakness?*

I reach deep inside to grasp the *yes* from my heart and pull it up out of my throat. I dig for the conviction behind my trembling consent. I look for the "me" who could be content not only with my weaknesses, but the insults, hardships, persecutions, and calamities they could and do bring into my life. All for the sake of Christ.

Much to my surprise, I am beginning to see that it requires much more strength to allow ourselves to be weak, and live with the repercussions of that weakness, than it does to be capable, competent, confident. To boast of the ways we are unable rather than the gifts and abilities Christ has granted us—what God would want that kind of disciple?

Our God would. Because He already has all the strength He needs. What He needs is a place to pour it out. And we are the conduits He longs to use to pass that power, that grace, that merciful love to the world. If we are already full and content in our own abilities, our own competence, then where is the space left for God to fill with His strength and power?

But if we will let ourselves be brought low by our weakness, then there is room for God to be lifted up. This, while it may seem a thorn in our own flesh, is an opportunity that our sweet Jesus relishes and delights in.

I am weak and fragile, and each day that I sit still in His Word and listen to what God has to say about that, I am more convinced that it is the most perfect way to be. If I am willing to offer fragility to Christ and to have the faith to believe He longs to use that weakness, He will pour His perfect strength through me like a living sieve. Holiness can be found here, if I will let the holes in my strength be outlets of His grace.

Colleen Mitchell

TO PONDER WITH YOUR PEN

Our weaknesses are as unique to our souls as our strengths. Even when we share common struggles, we each stumble and fall and push ourselves back up in our own way. Can you picture that sieve, with your unique holes? Draw it if you like, labeling each hole according to your own weakness. Now see the grace pouring through it? That is God, His power being made perfect in those weaknesses. If you'd prefer not to draw, your words are sufficient offerings to Him. Express your weaknesses and then call down His grace.

_____

_____

_____

_____

_____

_____

_____

_____

_____

_____

_____

_____

_____

_____

LIFTED TO THE LORD

Dear Lord, I am very much aware of the ways that I fall short of Your glory. Please increase my awareness of Your power perfected in my weaknesses.

day EIGHTEEN

PROVERBS 3:5-6 (NRSV-CE)

Trust in the Lord with all your heart,
   and do not rely on your own insight.
In all your ways acknowledge him,
   and he will make straight your paths.

For further reading: Isaiah 55:8-9, 1 Corinthians 13:10-12

THINK UPON THESE THINGS

We don't know. We just don't know. We want to control. We want to understand. We walk around puzzling it all out in our heads until we are sick with the weight and the motion of it all. But still, our own insight only gets us so far. More often than not, when we're honest, the things we worry most about, the things that have disappointed us the most, the things that rob our joy, are constructs of our own understanding. When God exhorts us not to lean on our own understanding, He's reminding us that our perceptions fall far short of omniscience. We don't know what we don't know. And it's been that way since the dawn of time.

God warned us not to eat of the Tree of Knowledge. It's not that He was opposed to our using and developing our intellect. On the contrary, God blessed us with our brains and He delights in our reason. He tells us that wisdom and understanding will make us happy. Faith and reason exist in perfectly happy harmony. One never contradicts the other. God loves reason.

However.

We are not to rely on our own insight. No matter how hard we study, how much experience we have, and who on earth we ask, our own insight will always be but a sliver of God's vast knowledge. We know, but only in part. God doesn't ever want us to be fooled into thinking we know it all or we know better than He does. That's why He warned Adam and Eve against the forbidden fruit. It's not knowledge that's a problem; it's how we take that knowledge and turn it around in our heads and then often end up wrestling it in our worry and despair. We weren't made to manipulate the things we think we know. We were made to trust.

But the fall left us forgetting. We forget that we are not omniscient. We forget that we are not wholly holy and often lack the irreproachability and wisdom to choose wisely. Finally, we are not nearly as powerful as we think we are. Only God can make plans conform to His will. We can't. Yet, we expend so much energy trying to do exactly that.

Do not rely on your own insight. Get out of your head.

Next time your intellect tempts you to lean exclusively on its strength, settle that fretting brain on the firm foundation of the Lord instead. Let Him bear it. His thoughts are higher. They are better. He sees this whole thing—whatever it is— much more clearly than you do.

Elizabeth Foss

TO PONDER WITH YOUR PEN

Copy the "further reading" verses here. Pray them into your heart.

_____

_____

_____

_____

_____

_____

_____

_____

_____

_____

_____

_____

_____

_____

_____

_____

_____

_____

_____

LIFTED TO THE LORD

I trust you, Lord and I believe that You know better than I do and that Your plans for life are all good. Help me to endure with hope and confidence the times I suffer, knowing that they can transform me into a truer likeness of You.

day NINETEEN

PSALM 46:10 (NRSV-CE)

Be still, and know that I am God. I am exalted among the nations, I am exalted in the earth.

For further reading: 1 Peter 5:6-11, 1 Chronicles 16:11

THINK UPON THESE THINGS

Did you ever stop to think what could be said about you in the first few days after you die? One of the greatest management principles going is to begin with the end in mind. I am not theologically astute enough to offer here an idea of what happens to a soul right after one dies, but I have to think that God is more concerned with the hidden moments of the heart than He is with the resume. The peace in leaving and the peace we leave are both about the way we loved when we still had time. I've written a few eulogies in the past couple of years: what people remember are the ways that you loved.

One day, someone will write our eulogies. Right now, we are writing our lives. From my perspective, in the front pews, with the people experiencing great loss, the lives best lived are the ones that seize all the little opportunities offered each one of us every day to stop and have a conversation, to offer our help, to serve in the smallest and least noticeable ways. What really defines the life of a truly great person are the decisions made to live a life that is a genuine expression of love.

What are your genuine expressions of love?

In those, we find our best strategy for living well. A healthy expression of our love isn't about *doing*; it's about surrendering. It isn't about achieving; it's about resting.

Those times we offer our achievements in exchange for love? They're bartering chips. Those are the areas of our self-affirming will. They make us anxious.

We have to be still and know God. We have to be still *to* know God.

Those times we still seek approval, still want worldly perfection, still climb? We aren't exalting God. We're offering ourselves and hoping that we will be exalted. There's no rest there. And there is no genuine love there.

When life bears down on me, my default mode is to put myself in drive and just keep going, working, organizing, multi-tasking. Inevitably, I end up in the confessional telling my spiritual director that I feel like my prayer life is suffering. And he looks me square in the eye and just says, "Martha, Martha. ... Be still and know that I am God."

When I remarked to a friend that I intended to make Psalm 46:10 my focus for a time, she reminded me that it's difficult for mothers to be still. Mothers are in perpetual motion. We are all about moving to meet a child's needs: rocking, swaddling, feeding, clothing, comforting, educating, driving everywhere. How, then, can we be still?

The NASB translation of Psalm 46:10 tells me to *stop striving* and know that He is God.

Striving: that tendency to put forth a great deal of effort trying to get everything perfect.

Striving depletes us. The best striving—our most earnest efforts—should be for seeking God. Your best efforts at excellence are all for naught if you are not earnestly endeavoring to seek the face of God first.

I wish I'd learned life's greatest lesson before middle age. I know there is no time in eternity and I console myself with that knowledge. Still. I wish I had learned.

I wish I knew then what I know now: God's love is not contingent on my performance. I can't earn it. He doesn't want me to strive for it. He wants me to rest in it. God made me. He loves me.

My heart was broken for a very long time. There was no real rest until it rested securely in the love of my Heavenly Father. When we rest securely in the arms of our Savior, we live by grace and we are truly free.

Grace.

It's grace we want. It's grace that restores us. It's grace that keeps us from crashing and burning again. Humility preserves peace and begets grace: the humility of knowing that we are little before God and entirely dependent upon Him and that we can rest assuredly in His goodness. That's the little way of peace.

We look to 1 Peter 5:6-11.

The woman who is humble before God will find grace for every trial and power to meet every assault of the devil. When we stop trying to do it all on our own and we literally surrender all our anxieties to Jesus, He meets us with grace enough for all. We let God be God. His grace is sufficient.

Do we live like we believe that?

We can. From this day forward we can live like all is grace.

Elizabeth Foss

TO PONDER WITH YOUR PEN

Saint Therese of Lisieux teaches us that everything is a grace, and every soul is tenderly loved. In *Story of a Soul*, she wrote,

> *He has created the great saints who are like the lilies and the roses, but He has also created much lesser saints and they must be content to be the daisies or the violets which rejoice His eyes whenever He glances down. Perfection consists in doing His will, in being that which He wants us to be. … The sun shines equally both on cedars and on every tiny flower. In just the same way God looks after every soul as if it had no equal. All is planned for the good of every soul, exactly as the seasons are so arranged that the humblest daisy blossoms at the appointed time.*

Pull out paints or colored pencils. Do you see yourself in the bouquet He gathers? Bring your images to Saint Therese's words.

LIFTED TO THE LORD

I love the daisies. I dearly love wildflowers that grow on the banks of the creek and herald the spring. And I know you love me infinitely more than I delight in these humble blooms. I turn my face Your Son, and I bask in the glorious light of Your love.

TWENTY

1 KINGS 19:1-10 (NRSV-CE)

Ahab told Jezebel all that Elijah had done, and how he had killed all the prophets with the sword. Then Jezebel sent a messenger to Elijah, saying, "So may the gods do to me, and more also, if I do not make your life like the life of one of them by this time tomorrow." Then he was afraid; he got up and fled for his life, and came to Beer-sheba, which belongs to Judah; he left his servant there.

But he himself went a day's journey into the wilderness, and came and sat down under a solitary broom tree. He asked that he might die: "It is enough; now, O Lord, take away my life, for I am no better than my ancestors." Then he lay down under the broom tree and fell asleep. Suddenly an angel touched him and said to him, "Get up and eat." He looked, and there at his head was a cake baked on hot stones, and a jar of water. He ate and drank, and lay down again. The angel of the Lord came a second time, touched him, and said, "Get up and eat, otherwise the journey will be too much for you." He got up, and ate and drank; then he went in the strength of that food forty days and forty nights to Horeb the mount of God. At that place he came to a cave, and spent the night there.

Then the word of the Lord came to him, saying, "What are you doing here, Elijah?" He answered, "I have been very zealous for the Lord, the God of hosts; for the Israelites have forsaken your covenant, thrown down your altars, and killed your prophets with the sword. I alone am left, and they are seeking my life, to take it away."

For further reading: 1 Corinthians 6:19-20, Genesis 1:29, Psalm 104:10-15

THINK UPON THESE THINGS

When I look at periods of burnout in my life, I can see certain patterns. There is always fatigue: I've pushed my body too far, too fast, for too long. There is always a transition: a baby, a move, a child leaving home, or a combination of these. There is always grief: loss, miscarriage, death. And there is always this issue with food.

I still remember the four pieces of penne I ate at my father-in-law's funeral. I knew there would be a price to pay. I'm absolutely unable to digest wheat. I knew I was risking a slide into inflammation and pain all over again. And I ate it anyway. Because I was too tired and too numb and too hungry to ask for the grace to walk to the salad at the end of the table.

Elijah is utterly burned out. He has been faithfully, fervently serving the Lord and he's overwhelmed and exhausted—so overwhelmed and exhausted that he can't even find the energy to feed himself. Here is a man of God, a man with an extraordinary prayer life (James 5:7-18), and a man just like us (well, if we were men). He has learned to pray well because he has learned that he cannot do life under his own power. He needs God. Elijah is a strong man who has learned dependence on His Creator. Still, he finds himself taking shelter under a broom tree, completely spent, and telling God he's had enough.

And the first thing God does with the situation is what every good Italian mother would do. God feeds Elijah. Actually, God sends an angel to feed Elijah. In our worlds, these angels are the "meal trains" of willing women who deliver food after a baby is born. They are the ladies at church who see to every detail of the funeral reception. They are my friend Martha, who showed up at my house with a memorable salad and a shoulder to cry on when no one was around after a miscarriage. They are the ministers of food.

Elijah's story speaks wisdom to me. I can hear the Lord prompting us to eat. He's not saying, "Go get donuts and coffee at the drive-thru." He's always reminding us that in our hardest moments, our bodies need real nourishment. Before we undertake the hard day, before we face another disappointment, we need to remember to get up and eat, otherwise the journey will be too much for us. If no angel appears to feed you, learn to feed yourself well, intentionally, with the purpose of nurturing. You cannot ignore the care and maintenance of the temple of the Holy Spirit and then expect it to be a beautiful, comfortable place to live. Eat well.

Even better, learn to eat sitting at a table, in community. We need to lift our weary heads from the stone and enter in, leaving behind the isolation of intense emotional pain and trading it for the ministry of compassion we can find at the table of friends. We need to learn to receive—food, drink, and love—from other people.

Then, nourished and rested, be on the lookout, always alert and aware, ready to bring food, ready to be the angel. Food is a love language. Learn to speak it well.

Elizabeth Foss

TO PONDER WITH YOUR PEN

Right now, make a grocery list. On it, list food that will nourish your body well, that will fill it with the goodness God provides for us in real food. Also, consider to whom you might deliver food. Would someone be cheered by a thoughtful gift of soup and bread, a carefully chosen basket of fruit? Nourish yourself and someone else today.

_____

_____

_____

_____

_____

_____

_____

_____

_____

_____

_____

_____

_____

_____

_____

_____

_____

LIFTED TO THE LORD
Dear God, Thank you for the food you graciously provide to me.
Strengthen me with its goodness and restore to me all that I need to
undertake the journey you've mapped out for me.

day
TWENTY-ONE

HIDE IT IN YOUR HEART

Today is a day to rest and be grateful. Take some time to look over your journaling from the week, to read a little more, to catch up on days when you didn't have as much time as you would have liked. Practice writing the memory verse here, and make it your own on the facing page.

Practice writing the verse here, and make it your own on the facing page.

1 PETER 5:10-11 (NRSV-CE)

And after you have suffered for a little while, the God of all grace, who has called you to his eternal glory in Christ, will himself restore, support, strengthen, and establish you. To him be the power forever and ever. Amen.

_____

_____

_____

_____

_____

_____

_____

_____

_____

_____

_____

_____

and after you have
suffered for a little while
the **God** of all grace
who has called you
to his eternal glory
in **Christ**
will himself
restore, support, strengthen
& establish you
to him be the power
forever and ever

Amen

1 PETER 5:10-11

TWENTY-TWO *day*

EPHESIANS 1: 3-14 (NRSV-CE)

Blessed be the God and Father of our Lord Jesus Christ, who has blessed us in Christ with every spiritual blessing in the heavenly places, just as he chose us in Christ before the foundation of the world to be holy and blameless before him in love. He destined us for adoption as his children through Jesus Christ, according to the good pleasure of his will, to the praise of his glorious grace that he freely bestowed on us in the Beloved. In him we have redemption through his blood, the forgiveness of our trespasses, according to the riches of his grace that he lavished on us. With all wisdom and insight he has made known to us the mystery of his will, according to his good pleasure that he set forth in Christ, as a plan for the fullness of time, to gather up all things in him, things in heaven and things on earth. In Christ we have also obtained an inheritance, having been destined according to the purpose of him who accomplishes all things according to his counsel and will, so that we, who were the first to set our hope on Christ, might live for the praise of his glory. In him you also, when you had heard the word of truth, the gospel of your salvation, and had believed in him, were marked with the seal of the promised Holy Spirit; this is the pledge of our inheritance toward redemption as God's own people, to the praise of his glory.

THINK UPON THESE THINGS

Earlier this year, I reached out to a dear friend and mentor for counsel as I recovered from an emotional collapse and a clinical diagnosis of a multi-faceted mental illness. She directed me to this Scripture and instructed me to visit it every day for a month, to spend time with it, and she said strongly, "Do *not* journal."

I was taken aback. Obviously, journaling is an important part of praying for me. "But," I stammered, "that's how I pray!"

"I know," she responded, "but not right now. I want you to be uncomfortable long enough that you get out of your head and into your heart while you pray." This was an unexpected challenge, but I had reached out to this woman for her wisdom, and I trusted her guidance.

For a full month, every day, I sat with these words. My hand twitched with the instinct to grab a pen. I was distracted, unsure what I was supposed to be getting out of this exercise. And then, I began to hear.

Blameless spoken over me. *Destined in love to be his [daughter]. Grace which he bestowed freely on us.* I would turn on praise music as I washed the dishes and hear it again in familiar songs. *Blameless. His. Grace freely given.* And I realized how much I needed those words to be written on my heart.

What I learned in that month was that I had begun to question my very makeup, and that I was carrying around a heavy weight of self-blame for my current circumstances. After all, who lets herself fall so far into burnout that she completely collapses? I knew better. I should have done better.

Could it be that God would still choose me as His own, choose to use me, if I had messed things up this badly? And if *I* was this badly messed up? These were questions I did not even know I was wrestling with until He began to speak the answers over me. I realized I needed desperately to hear my Father say that I was His, that He had chosen me even before He had moved over the earth. I was set free from the burden of shame at my state of brokenness when I heard the promise of His lavish grace, given freely in great love for me, in the person of His Son. And finally, after a long month of listening, I could hear His voice of compassion and mercy calling me *blameless*.

Sometimes we don't know what our hearts need until we sit long enough to hear it. Often, in our striving for holiness, we forget that God is lavishly offering His grace to get us there. Perhaps, like me, you carry the burden of self-blame for your struggles. There is an invitation here for you. You are welcome to linger in these words until you hear His promises and are set free from burdens you might not even know you are bearing.

Colleen Mitchell

TO PONDER WITH YOUR PEN

Nothing. Do nothing with your hands today. Instead, sit still. Listen. Let the words sink in.

LIFTED TO THE LORD

Dear God, Thank you for the food you graciously provide to me. Strengthen me with its goodness and restore to me all that I need to undertake the journey you've mapped out for me.

TWENTY-THREE *day*

ROMANS 8:38-39 (NRSV-CE)

For I am convinced that neither death, nor life, nor angels, nor rulers, nor things present, nor things to come, nor powers, nor height, nor depth, nor anything else in all creation, will be able to separate us from the love of God in Christ Jesus our Lord.

For further reading: John 16:29-33

THINK UPON THESE THINGS

One of my favorite scenes from the must-see movie *The Princess Bride* takes place on the top of a hill. Buttercup is arguing with the Man in Black, believing that he is not Westley, her love, but the man who killed him, the Dread Pirate Roberts. The Man in Black is toying with her about how much she supposedly loved Westley, and she screams, "You mock my pain!" And Westley/Dread Pirate Roberts replies, "Life is pain, highness. Anyone who says differently is selling something."

This pronouncement is not something I generally like to hear when I'm in deep discomfort, but after I've had a few moments (hours…days…) of denial and self-pity, it is a truism to which I continually return. This life *is* pain. It will knock the wind out of you right when a deep breath is most needed, and it can seem terribly, absolutely, cruelly unfair. As I struggle through my hardest times—the loss of a parent, the shame of letting someone down, the weight of a large career decision, the fog of mental and physical sickness—more bad things seem to happen. I get into a car accident, every kitchen appliance breaks, grades plummet, a close friend contemplates taking her life. I catch myself staring at the sky asking, *Why God? Really? Is there any more we can pile on to the top of this case?*

Even if we *know* that God might be the best person to invite to join us in our mess, it can be so easy to push Him away during these times. We can feel very abandoned, and that is a lonely, desperate, deeply soul-shattering place to be. Just like Buttercup, we push our greatest love down the hill.

Here is where God's unending love for us kicks in. He has gifted us with the free will to push Him away. As we do, He tells us without malice and with the immediate capacity to forgive: "As you wish."

And then I'm Buttercup, left at the top of the hill alone, and suddenly I'm realizing what I've been pushing away in my despair. I've been shutting out His unfailing love. I realize I can tumble down this hill, thorns and all, if He's doing it with me. I'm left thanking God that He is much better at loving than I am. Our hope for making it through life's hardest trials is not in us; it's in Him.

Because here's the reality, or at least my reality: Life is pain, highness. But nothing, *nothing*, neither death nor life, nor things present nor things to come, nor a thousand bloodhounds nor a thousand swords, can break God's love for us. Since

He loves us, God will not give us a challenge that we cannot handle, because we don't have to handle it alone. His love will carry us through it.

He tells us, "Take courage; I have conquered the world." Have hope in that, sisters. He's done this a few times. Let Him guide you through this pain. Let Him hold you in his hands. He truly, madly, deeply loves you, and He will not abandon you. As you wish.

Katy Greiner

TO PONDER WITH YOUR PEN

There you are, at the top of the hill, alone. See what you've been pushing away? Call Him back. Tell Him you need Him and pour out to Him all the reasons You do. Spill it all. Then, when you've finished pouring out every angst, write "He Will Conquer" across that page. Use watercolor or a highlighter if you want to preserve a record of what you offered to Him. Just know that when you look back, you will see that He was on that hill with you, Buttercup.

LIFTED TO THE LORD

Jesus, You are real and living in my life. I am thankful that in my moments of overwhelming despair, I can call out to you, even if, at first, it is to whine about the torrent of sorrow falling on me. Thank You for being patient with me, and for standing at the bottom of the hill, waiting for me to invite You up. I need You. Please come carry me down safely.

TWENTY-FOUR *day*

MATTHEW 14:28-33 (NRSV-CE)

Peter answered him, "Lord, if it is you, command me to come to you on the water." He said, "Come." So Peter got out of the boat, started walking on the water, and came toward Jesus. But when he noticed the strong wind, he became frightened, and beginning to sink, he cried out, "Lord, save me!" Jesus immediately reached out his hand and caught him, saying to him, "You of little faith, why did you doubt?" When they got into the boat, the wind ceased. And those in the boat worshiped him, saying, "Truly you are the Son of God."

For Further Reading: Isaiah 41

THINK UPON THESE THINGS

She knew how to ride that two-wheeler and Granddad knew that she knew. He knew that she was strong and stable and balanced perfectly above two small wheels with hot pink spokes. So, he held the back of her seat and jogged along beside her, and then, he let go. She panicked, and as she jerked her head wildly, her arms followed along. So did the front end of her bike, already a bit unstable due to a loose bolt. She crashed into the mailbox. Poor Granddad looked at the crumpled heap of little girl and Barbie bike and said, "If only I'd gotten out in front of her, so she could see me while she pedaled the straightaway alone."

In Sacred Scripture, there are at least eighty reminders not to fear. God knew that human beings are prone to anxiety. He knew we'd need to be reminded to trust Him over and over again as we turned the pages of our Bibles and read about the fears of the people of God. So, He showed us how He spoke to them and acted on their behalf. We see without exception how faithfully He met them in the places of dismay.

Isaiah 41 shows us a full blueprint of God's provision against fear. The Lord commands us not to fear and then not to worry. He shows us His faithfulness and inspires in us a confidence necessary to follow His commands. It is interesting to note the variety of translations for that small phrase in Isaiah 41:10.

do not be dismayed (RSV)
turn not aside (Douay-Rheims)
do not be anxious (NAB)
do not anxiously look about you (NASB)
do not be afraid (CSB)

So many ways to say that we really need to keep our eyes fixed on God and trust! Just keep pedaling, straight and steady, eyes on the strong presence that will protect.

Careful study of Isaiah 41 calls out the reasons to know we can be at peace. God is with us and He will strengthen us. He promises to help us. He will always be the Lord of our lives. And He will uphold us, bracing us against the trials of this world. The promises in Isaiah 41 are pillars, a firm support system of belief. When we build our lives on these pillars, we let Him fortify us against attacks of darkness.

God knows we will fear; He knows we'll be overwhelmed by the storms. Even the saints trembled on the verge of utter despair. Saint Thomas More, in prison awaiting certain execution, wrote to his daughter, "I will not mistrust Him, Meg, although I shall feel myself weakening and on the verge of being overcome with fear. I shall remember how St. Peter at a blast of wind began to sink because of his lack of faith, and I shall do as he did: call upon Christ and pray to Him for help. And then I trust He shall place His holy hand on me and in the stormy seas hold me up from drowning."

Remember Saint Peter on the water in the wind? It was when he doubted that he began to sink. As he looked anxiously about, and took his eyes off Christ, the waves began to overwhelm him. As soon as he fixed his eyes—and his faith—back on the Savior, as soon as he called out to the Lord with confidence, Jesus reached out His hand and caught Him.

That's what God does. He catches us. He holds us up. He supports us in the storms.

Elizabeth Foss

TO PONDER WITH YOUR PEN

It is helpful to keep a record of God's faithfulness. Today, take some time to remember that He was with you, to recount how He calmed the storms and how you found yourself safely back in the boat, more aware of the power of God.

_____

_____

_____

_____

_____

_____

_____

_____

_____

_____

_____

_____

_____

_____

_____

_____

LIFTED TO THE LORD

I see you, Lord, there beside me. When I am tempted to jerk my head wildly, panicking because I think I am alone and vulnerable, bring me into Your presence. Let me fix my eyes on You.

TWENTY-FIVE *day*

LUKE 10:38-42 (NRSV-CE)

Now as they went on their way, he entered a certain village, where a woman named Martha welcomed him into her home. She had a sister named Mary, who sat at the Lord's feet and listened to what he was saying. But Martha was distracted by her many tasks; so she came to him and asked, "Lord, do you not care that my sister has left me to do all the work by myself? Tell her then to help me." But the Lord answered her, "Martha, Martha, you are worried and distracted by many things; there is need of only one thing. Mary has chosen the better part, which will not be taken away from her."

THINK UPON THESE THINGS

Today, I deep cleaned my house. It was in anticipation of a dear friend, who was visiting for the first time in months. He was traveling from out of town, and I wanted everything to be perfect for his arrival. I washed dishes, swept the stairs, ran loads of laundry, and picked up every fast food bag abandoned by my housemates.

I went in with good intentions; I wanted to make our home beautiful again, but grew more and more frustrated with every mess I encountered. I am blessed to live with four wonderful humans who make me laugh every day. However, we aren't always careful of where we leave messes. I've grown to know them very well, down to an ability to recognize who ate what for lunch based on the take-out box forgotten on the coffee table. It didn't help that my roommates were just as excited to welcome our guest, but didn't make an effort to reconcile our house. My anger at my roommates mounted throughout the day, until I realized how much I was parodying the parable in today's verse. I was Martha. I am so often Martha. But wouldn't we rather be Mary?

When my guest arrived, I was still busy in the kitchen, slicing bread. I gave a quick hello and returned to my task. There I was again, missing the point. All day, I waited and waited for him to arrive, only to gloss over his entrance and return to my priority. I should have dropped it all and immediately welcomed him into my home. I know him, I know his heart, and I know he couldn't care less what my house looked like when he walked in the door. He just wanted to see us.

I grew up in a household that overflowed with hospitality. Even if it was just one friend stopping by for coffee, my mother would compile a spread of food so delicious and elaborate, that I would immediately reach to invite others to join. She has a desire to feed every person who comes through our house, every friend of her children, every relative and neighbor. In high school, my house was always filled with plates of meats and cheese and pastries. The tea kettle was so often used, it hardly ever cooled. We would sit around our kitchen table and rid ourselves of the stress from school or relationships or uncertainty about the future. And that is how I learned to define hospitality.

It's okay if the table doesn't get set in time (or even at all). It's even okay if what you can provide is modest. A cup of tea. A handful of crackers or cookies. The intent is not to impress a guest, but to unburden them. To give them a space in which they can breathe and laugh and rest.

It doesn't take an out-of-town guest to recognize that acts of service can become expressions of vanity. It's easy to aim to please, but the root of the aim isn't always clear or pure. As women of faith, we are often presented with opportunities to serve. How we approach that service defines us. When you are called upon, first offer it up. As you load the dishwasher or make the bed, think of Whom you are truly honoring through your actions. Forgive your children, your husband, your roommate for creating that last little mess. Know that that your presence, your being, and your peace are truly what those around you seek. Allow yourself to rest into a conversation around the table. Listen, and listen well, with your whole heart, knowing that hospitality is housed in a person and not a place.

Carly Buckholz

TO PONDER WITH YOUR PEN

How often are you troubled about many things and yet, that trouble is really what you've manufactured in your own head as you've worried about being "perfect?" The anxiety of perfection nestles into the heart of vanity. There is a frenzied fervor to find our worth in the way other people perceive us, and that energy can make us anxious indeed. Write yourself a letter. Give yourself permission to just be "good enough," especially when "good enough" makes you more available for occasions of genuine camaraderie and friendship.

_____

_____

_____

_____

_____

_____

_____

_____

_____

_____

_____

_____

_____

_____

LIFTED TO THE LORD
Lord, I am grateful for the moments when I sit at your feet, content to know that there is no other place You'd have me be, no other company You'd want me to keep. When I serve you, let me serve from this place, secure in Your teaching, and free from the anxiety of anyone else's expectations or perceptions.

TWENTY-SIX *day*

ISAIAH 45:5-8 (NRSV-CE)

I am the Lord, and there is no other;
   besides me there is no god.
   I arm you, though you do not know me,
so that they may know, from the rising of the sun
   and from the west, that there is no one besides me;
   I am the Lord, and there is no other.
I form light and create darkness,
   I make weal and create woe;
   I the Lord do all these things.
Shower, O heavens, from above,
   and let the skies rain down righteousness;
let the earth open, that salvation may spring up,
   and let it cause righteousness to sprout up also;
   I the Lord have created it.

For further reading: Jeremiah 12: 7-10, Isaiah 64: 7-8, Luke 23: 44-46

THINK UPON THESE THINGS

Those first verses from Isaiah are tough ones to tackle. I've seen them come to life, the pain in my boy's eyes palpable even in the distance between us across a kitchen counter. They flash with injured accusation: *If God is creator of all things, then God made evil as well as good.*

But, but, but, I stammer and try to sort this in my head. *God is infinitely good.*

How then, do we reconcile the infinitely good God with the maker of "weal" and "woe?"

There can be no doubt that God tests us and His tests are painful and those testing times are full of woe. Men have been wrestling to reconcile a good God with the pain of suffering for as long as there have been tears. Origen, the most noted theologian of the early Greek Church, posits that God wants to convert men by their suffering. He is the Great Physician. Please remember that surgeries and chemotherapy are difficult and painful and evoke suffering—but no one blames the doctor.

St. Gregory the Great comments that in the moment when created things cause us to suffer, God offers his peace. "Our union with God is broken by sin; it is fitting, therefore, that we return to him along the path of suffering. When any created thing causes us to suffer, it is an instrument for our conversion, so that we will return humbly to the source of peace" (*Moralia in Job* 3, 9, 15).

There is a devil that prowls the world, intent on pulling us from God. Our good God allows him to exist amongst us. This is so hard to reconcile. God knows that He can bring about our full conversion through trials and temptations. He knows that the evil one will try to make us abandon the path to heaven, will delight in our throwing up our hands and shouting in anger or sorrow, "It's too hard! God has abandoned me!" In that moment, Jesus, from the cross, groans with us. He knows. He knows how hard suffering is. When it is too hard, when we have come to the end of ourselves and we are fully spent, we look to heaven with our Savior and we commend our spirit to the Father.

We live this life on earth in a certain tension between the fallen world and the life He promises. We wrestle with our dreams and our disappointments. Discerning desires, sifting sorrows, we find ourselves wondering if our longing is inspired by the will of God or if it is the symptom of our brokenness. We suffer. Sometimes we suffer nearly to the point of death. He brings us to the end of ourselves, and we are so tempted to curse Him and give up on the life of nearness to God. We are humbled and bent low.

In this dark place, this descent into utter sorrow, our souls are soft and pliable; our Maker takes them gently in His hands. We make a small move and incline ourselves towards our God. We offer the formless mess of our muddy self to Him to fashion into a likeness of Himself. A humble and contrite heart can be made like the Lord's. Tenderly, the Potter sculpts a masterpiece of the now shapeless mass that has been kneaded by suffering and sorrow. Tenderly, we are restored to the life He intends for us.

Elizabeth Foss

TO PONDER WITH YOUR PEN

Move towards God today. Hear Him groan with you. Whatever your sufferings, whether big or small, see that He knows your pain. Understand that He longs to make your heart like His. Humble yourself. Confess your transgressions. Surrender your weaknesses.

LIFTED TO THE LORD

You are the infinitely good God. Even weal and woe are used by You for my good. Please take my sufferings and make them instruments of my heart's conversion.

TWENTY-SEVEN *day*

MATTHEW 11:28-30 (NRSV-CE)

"Come to me, all you that are weary and are carrying heavy burdens, and I will give you rest. Take my yoke upon you, and learn from me; for I am gentle and humble in heart, and you will find rest for your souls. For my yoke is easy, and my burden is light."

ISAIAH 30:15 (NRSV-CE)

For thus said the Lord God, the Holy One of Israel:
In returning and rest you shall be saved;
   in quietness and in trust shall be your strength.

For further reading: Psalm 127:1-2, Mark 6:30-32, Exodus 34:21

THINK UPON THESE THINGS

I will never forget that weekend in my big family. Without betraying confidences or telling stories that aren't mine to tell: we visited emergency rooms in two towns, we nursed 104 degree fevers in a third, we helped a young family begin their move to a new home 3,000 miles away by bringing them home to our house first, we handled a serious emotional health crisis, we watched a grown child say goodbye to his brother's family before they left for California and say goodbye to his grandmother before she went home to heaven, and we discussed with loved ones what the final hospice days would hold.

It was a weekend so far beyond my wildest imaginings. So many things—big things—all at the same time. I looked blearily at my husband that Sunday night as he handed me a piece of chocolate. I shook my head, "No, thank you. Hey, what did you give up for Lent?"

"Fun," came his reply. "And sleep."

I put my head in my hands and asked myself what in the world we were doing wrong to feel so off balance and so exhausted.

That was an extreme season in our lives, but there have been others. There was the end of the semester when I wondered why I thought 18 credit hours was a good idea. There was the nursing of a toddler and a newborn following a C-section. There is the round-the-clock rhythm of life with four teenagers, two young children, and a revolving door of college kids.

This is life. It makes you tired. But strength is restored in quiet and rest. When we are tired, everything is more difficult. We are more likely to complain, to lose perspective, to lose our tempers. These creeping manifestations of easily tripped triggers are clear signs to rest. This isn't the time for deep introspection. It's time for a nap.

Women often operate under the mistaken notion that if we just manage time better—if we can multi-task with the best of them—we'll triumph over the natural limitations of a 24-hour day and a seven-day week. Rarely do we consider that our Creator intended for us to sleep for a third of that day and to devote one of those seven days entirely to rest. God asks you to take up your cross, but He also clearly tells you to take *only* the burden He designed for you. His intended yoke won't wear you down into a blubbering (and sinful) mess. Remember, His yoke is easy and light, but He intended you to carry it only after sleeping, and after taking Sundays for restoration and the reception of grace and strength He offers in the Eucharist.

No one is going to rest for you. No one but you can take the responsibility for nurturing your body in order to restore your soul. We are all tired, but we are tired in different ways and our ways to rest will vary, too.

Women across generations hold in common the desolate sense of loss that comes with sleep deprivation. It utterly depletes us. Any effort to amend our ways—to be more efficient or better managers of anything—is defeated before it's begun if it is undertaken by a weary body and soul. We want to find our way back to healthy and whole happiness. For the exhausted, the only path there is the act of surrender that comes when we rest.

Trust.

You don't keep the world spinning; God does. And He will most certainly continue to do that while you take a nap.

Elizabeth Foss

WITH YOUR HANDS

How do you nurture yourself through rest? How can you do more of those things?
Journal awhile about rest and what makes it work and what keeps you from it.
Then, go make your bed and plump your pillows and do what you can to prepare
your sleeping environment, so that when it's time for sleep, you'll be happy to find
yourself there.

_____

_____

_____

_____

_____

_____

_____

_____

_____

_____

_____

_____

_____

_____

_____

_____

LIFTED TO THE LORD

Thank You for the gift of rest. Help me to find faith to surrender to You
and allow myself to sleep. Make me ever aware that You are the One
upon whom the world and every little thing in it depends, not me.

day TWENTY-EIGHT

HIDE IT IN YOUR HEART

Today is a day to rest and be grateful. Take some time to look over your journaling from the week, to read a little more, to catch up on days when you didn't have as much time as you would have liked. Practice writing the memory verse here, and make it your own on the facing page.

Practice writing the verse here, and make it your own on the facing page.

MATTHEW 11:28 (NRSV-CE)

Come to me, all you that are weary and are carrying heavy burdens, and I will give you rest.

_____

_____

_____

_____

_____

_____

_____

_____

_____

_____

_____

_____

_____

come
to me, all who are
weary & carrying
heavy
burdens
and i will give you
rest

MATTHEW 11:28

TWENTY-NINE *day*

1 JOHN 3:14 (NRSV-CE)

We know that we have passed from death to life because we love one another. Whoever does not love abides in death.

JOHN 5: 24 (NRSV-CE)

Very truly, I tell you, anyone who hears my word and believes him who sent me has eternal life, and does not come under judgment, but has passed from death to life.

For further reading: John 3:16, John 11:25-26

THINK UPON THESE THINGS

I used to live in fear of death. I'd lie awake at night, worrying about when it would come. Anxious that I wouldn't have time to accomplish everything I wanted to do, I obsessively pursued goals, always striving for perfection. And I tried to control other aspects of my life as much as possible, making meticulous plans and striving to ensure that everyone had a positive perception of me.

But then, I was diagnosed with an aggressive form of cancer, and my fear became real. None of the time I had spent worrying and none of the goals I had accomplished made the news any easier to handle. The illusion of control I had so carefully constructed crumbled in an instant.

Because I was pregnant, I couldn't start treatment until after my son was delivered. The day before the C-section, my family surprised me with a baby shower. It was heart-wrenching to hold onesies and tiny socks while acutely aware that my son might never wear them or that I might not be the one to dress him. In my sorrow, I prayed, *God, I want to live and hold my baby. But this is in Your hands.*

Let thy will be done, I added, hoping He would strengthen me to truly mean those words.

That night, I slept soundly. Amidst chaotic surgery prep the next morning, I was calm. And as the anesthesia took hold, I was at peace. When I should have most feared death, I felt no fear; God's grace filled me with the faith to trust in the promise of eternal life.

I live differently now. Instead of chasing what it *seems* I should do and demanding perfection, I pursue what makes me feel alive, even when it means risking failure. I've loosened my grip on the plans I have for my life, because I trust that God's plans are greater and that He wants only good for me. I no longer obsess over other people's perceptions of me, and I try to embrace the woman God created me to be—flaws and all. I no longer fear death, but take comfort in the promise of eternal life and trust that God will once again fill me with peace when my time to die comes.

Whether we've flirted with death or not, we can choose to live in freedom because Jesus told us He is the Son of God, He died for our sins on the cross, and He promised that if we believe in the One who sent Him, we will have eternal life. Let's break through the chains of fear and trust His word. Let's live in the true freedom He offers us. Saint Catherine of Siena said, "Be who God meant you to be and you will set the world on fire." Let's not waste time worrying how long our candle will burn, but rather work to keep it continuously ablaze, shining the light of Christ as God created us to do.

Allison McGinley

TO PONDER WITH YOUR PEN

In the rhythm of everyday life, we often lose sight of the extraordinary gift that is an ordinary day. An awareness of life's fragility makes us grateful to be alive every morning. A fear of dying debilitates us. Think about your mornings and the rhythms of your everyday life. How can you greet the day in a way that honors the gift that it is?

_____

_____

_____

_____

_____

_____

_____

_____

_____

_____

_____

_____

_____

_____

_____

_____

_____

LIFTED TO THE LORD

Dear Lord, I offer You this morning, ever so grateful to be alive. Please guard my heart against the fears that blind me to the gift of a new day. Let your Spirit grow in me, making me increasingly thankful for the precious gift of life, and, living in the freedom of knowing Your plans are better than mine, help me to truly embrace the life You want for me.

THIRTY *day*

MATTHEW 6: 19-24 (NRSV-CE)

"Do not store up for yourselves treasures on earth, where moth and rust consume and where thieves break in and steal; but store up for yourselves treasures in heaven, where neither moth nor rust consumes and where thieves do not break in and steal. For where your treasure is, there your heart will be also.

"The eye is the lamp of the body. So, if your eye is healthy, your whole body will be full of light; but if your eye is unhealthy, your whole body will be full of darkness. If then the light in you is darkness, how great is the darkness!

"No one can serve two masters; for a slave will either hate the one and love the other, or be devoted to the one and despise the other. You cannot serve God and wealth."

For further reading: Psalm 37:1-9, 21-26

THINK UPON THESE THINGS

When I was a little girl I had a special box for all my little treasures and trinkets. There was my favorite marble with swirls of pink and white, a sheet of scratch and sniff stickers, my rainbow pencil, a ballerina candle holder from my fifth birthday, a teddy bear keychain a friend at school had given me, and the mini Strawberry Shortcake doll that I had obsessed over in the Sears catalog until one birthday, it magically appeared among my presents and I thought I'd died and gone to heaven. I held tightly to those little treasures and protected them like a Mama Bear would her cub. My six brothers didn't have a clue as to where I hid my treasures since I would move my box every night to ensure its safety from the marauding thieves who lived with me. It was important to me to protect what was mine and only mine.

One day I had hidden the box so well, I could not find it. My ten-year-old self was crushed. I wept and wailed at the loss of such precious treasure. My mother tried her best to console my broken heart, but I knew without a doubt that life was over. Mom tried to explain that any gift given in love still had value even when that physical gift was broken or lost. It was the love that was important. *Love, schmove!* I told her. I knew I'd never have anything that special again. My treasures were gone forever, and I was devastated.

A decade or two later, after I married and my husband and I had just welcomed our first child, my mom called to say she had found my long-lost treasure box. She wanted to know what to do with it. It made me pause for a moment. I looked down at my sleeping son, snuggled safe in my arms, and understood in that moment what my real treasure was.

Love.

It was always about love. I had placed such importance on those special treasures that without them, I felt lost. Here I was holding the most beautiful miracle, and I could not imagine my world without him. I now understood what my mother meant when she'd counseled so long ago that instead of holding onto things, I needed to hold onto the love these things represented. The love is what was important.

In today's reading, Matthew encourages us to not store up treasures here on earth, but to strive for treasures in heaven. To be generous with our time, talent, and treasure. To serve with joy knowing that "For where your treasure is, there will your heart be also."

My heart was in my arms, a gift from my Father above who loved me more than I could ever fully comprehend. My son was not a bank balance, a pair of diamond earrings, or a Strawberry Shortcake doll. He was so much more important than anything that little treasure box contained. God gave Jerry and me our son in order to show us how to love and to give of ourselves until it hurt. He gave us our son in order to teach us how to treasure God.

Mary Lenaburg

TO PONDER WITH YOUR PEN

Are you anxiously protecting treasures on earth? Can you embrace the freedom that comes with relinquishing them and investing your heart with love instead?

_____

_____

_____

_____

_____

_____

_____

_____

_____

_____

_____

_____

_____

_____

_____

_____

_____

LIFTED TO THE LORD

Dear Lord, help me to let go of the worried grip I have on things and reach out with open hands to what You would have me hold instead.

THIRTY-ONE *day*

ISAIAH 64:8 (NRSV-CE)

Yet, O Lord, you are our Father;
  we are the clay, and you are our potter;
  we are all the work of your hand.

For further reading: Psalm 138: 7-8, Philippians 1:6

THINK UPON THESE THINGS

All night, I had watched them move like ribbons. He gestured when he talked, waving his hands around for emphasis. Later, on the dim patio, he moved them into the light so I could look closer. The skin was peeled back in some parts, revealing pink flesh. The patches of raw contrasted with the otherwise smooth and tan. He had spent the previous week at the beach. The sun had done a number on his hands alone, tearing them apart with burns of multiple degrees. Now, I watched him trace the parts of his missing skin, like maps splayed out beneath the knuckles. "Will they heal?" I asked, unsure if it was touching a nerve, following only where I had seen his own fingers brush. "I hope," he said, "these don't look familiar anymore."

And I thought, *how often I forgot to appreciate my own.* How central my hands are to my livelihood. How instrumental our hands are to our daily actions; we stare at their backs as we type all day, cup them as we cradle an infant, use our fingers to come through the hair of a child, knead dough for rosemary bread. We lift windows to let in spring air. We clutch steering wheels, turn doorknobs to welcome loved ones into our home.

At seventeen, I went on a pilgrimage with my youth group through Italy and Spain. While in Rome, we visited a monastery for adoration. I was overwhelmed, the day hanging heavy on my shoulders. Travel had tired me to the point where my thoughts weren't fluid, when prayer seemed even less accessible. I busied myself by glancing around the room, set on waiting out the hour by distractions rather than adoration. My eye caught on a woman in the pew a few rows ahead. Her head was bowed, her serene face barely visible through the curtain of hair that had shifted from behind her shoulders. I watched as she began to mouth, *Come, Holy Spirit,* over and over and over. I watched as she lifted her hands, turned her wrists, and cupped them together, as if asking for God's grace to overflow. Peacefully waiting for the Spirit to arrive. I wanted that; I wanted that serenity and patience. Slowly, my hands rose, palms up, head bowed. *Come, Holy Spirit.* At times in prayer, concentration seems to be on the far side of the shore. My mind stumbles through thoughts and trivial tasks, unable to breathe easy in the small adoration chapel. The quiet moment in Rome has become my default, my first position of prayer. When my mind is spinning too quickly to listen, the repetition of the call to the Spirit slows me down, centers me, allows for a space in which God can speak.

Today, we consider the hands of a potter, an artist whose creations are truly larger than life. We are the work of those hands. We are the clay, ready to be pushed and pulled and molded into creation. We are blessed with a master Craftsman to guide us through all tasks and worries and triumphs. Turn out your hands. Lift them and show them to the Lord, every ebb and flow of your skin. Every vein and estuary. Every scar and burn and blemish. Do not forsake the work of them. Appreciate their ability to love, to nurture, to care. Allow His hands to guard you and guide you. Trust that He will deliver you into perfection.

Carly Buckholz

TO PONDER WITH YOUR PEN

Sit for a few quiet moments and look at closely at your hands. See the tales they tell in the scars they bear? What a gift our hands are—the tools we use to care for ourselves and to interact with one another. How do you use your hands as God's instruments? How does He bless you with your very own hands?

_____

_____

_____

_____

_____

_____

_____

_____

_____

_____

_____

_____

_____

_____

_____

_____

LIFTED TO THE LORD

You are the Potter who has sculpted me into Your image. Make me
mindful of that truth as I move in the world today. Let me hands—
and my heart—be truly Yours.

THIRTY-TWO *day*

MARK 14: 32-36 (NRSV-CE)

They went to a place called Gethsemane; and he said to his disciples, "Sit here while I pray." He took with him Peter and James and John, and began to be distressed and agitated. And he said to them, "I am deeply grieved, even to death; remain here, and keep awake." And going a little farther, he threw himself on the ground and prayed that, if it were possible, the hour might pass from him. He said, "Abba, Father, for you all things are possible; remove this cup from me; yet, not what I want, but what you want."

For further reading: Luke 22:39-42, Matthew 26:37-39

THINK UPON THESE THINGS

We all have the moment; we all experience a time that stands forever frozen in memory. I remember what we were eating for dinner the night my father told us he was leaving. I remember the expression on my husband's face when he first saw the CT scans, confirming I had cancer. I remember the chill that coursed through my veins while I stood in the produce section at Trader Joe's and took a phone call which informed me that my child was in dire need.

Those are the moments that test our faith, threaten to shake us to the foundation, revealing cracks in our peace. Those are the moments that can, and frequently do, cause despondency. Even Jesus had His moment. Maybe especially Jesus had His moment—that deliberate time so important to us now that it was recounted in three of the four gospels. Jesus knew that He was going to suffer a terrible death. In that moment—His moment of vulnerability—He showed us what to do. If we can watch carefully and learn from Him, we take from His moment the tools we need to better manage ours.

Jesus chose His dearest friends to be with Him. He didn't throw Himself into a crowd and stuff His feelings, nor did curl up in a ball by Himself. (I think it's also safe to assume that He would not have spent mindless hours scrolling social media, comparing Himself to edited images on the Internet.) Instead, he gathered His inner circle and drew away with them. He confided in them, lowered His guard, let them in on His vulnerability. He said it aloud: I'm deeply grieved, even to death, and I need you to stay with me. He teaches us to speak the words of our need aloud to people we can trust.

Jesus asked His friends to pray with Him, to engage in the fierce spiritual warfare that is set before them all. He's warned them that the time will come when they're tempted to be deeply troubled, but He also told them that even when it looks like all is lost they need to remember His way will look different from what they expect. He has already said, "Peace I leave with you; my peace I give to you. I do not give to you as the world gives. Do not let your hearts be troubled, and do not let them be afraid" (John 14:27). He wanted them to keep vigil in hope. When life presents us with our moment and the devil is wresting for control, fighting with every fiber of his being to pull us away from God and challenge our belief, God tells us to find our small cluster of good friends who will pray for us with hope.

Still, in His moment, Jesus was unbearably sorrowful. Jesus—God Himself—was so distraught that He sweat blood. It occurs to me that it was probably not helpful that His friends had fallen asleep on the job. Such is life. There is no one on this planet who can walk every moment of pain with us. Some of those moments, we walk alone, imploring the Father to take the cup of suffering from us. Jesus cried out to His Father, begging Him to overcome the pain of evil, all the while knowing that He most certainly would triumph. Jesus put His soul in His Father's capable hands, coming to a peaceful surrender into the will of God.

We all have our moments of despair. If you live long enough, there will certainly be more than one such moment. There will be times when, if we squeeze our eyes tightly enough against the pain, we can almost see the forces of good and evil battling it out, Satan trying to plunge us over the cliff of despair into utter desolation and depression. Those are the moments when we walk with Jesus in Gethsemane, when we gather our beloved friends, when we kneel alone before the Father, when we surrender to His will, and when we trust that He is truly the ultimate victor over pain.

Elizabeth Foss

TO PONDER WITH YOUR PEN

When you are troubled, where do you retreat to be with the Lord? Where do you go—either physically or mentally—to sit and stay awake with Him in suffering? Which saints are there with you? How do they help you keep watch?

_____

_____

_____

_____

_____

_____

_____

_____

_____

_____

_____

_____

_____

_____

_____

_____

LIFTED TO THE LORD

I am here, Lord, in Your presence, in the garden of suffering. I know
that You never sleep. Be with me now.

THIRTY-THREE *day*

MATTHEW 4: 18-22 (NRSV-CE)

As he walked by the Sea of Galilee, he saw two brothers, Simon, who is called Peter, and Andrew his brother, casting a net into the sea—for they were fishermen. And he said to them, "Follow me, and I will make you fish for people." Immediately they left their nets and followed him. As he went from there, he saw two other brothers, James son of Zebedee and his brother John, in the boat with their father Zebedee, mending their nets, and he called them. Immediately they left the boat and their father, and followed him.

MATTHEW 5:29-30 (NRSV-CE)

If your right eye causes you to sin, tear it out and throw it away; it is better for you to lose one of your members than for your whole body to be thrown into hell. And if your right hand causes you to sin, cut it off and throw it away; it is better for you to lose one of your members than for your whole body to go into hell.

For further reading: John 13:4-14

THINK UPON THESE THINGS

I awaken much too early, insomnia propping my eyes wide open. Downstairs on the couch, I push a button and light the still-dark early morning. Instantly, I am in the worlds of other women. I see babies—lots of babies. I see meals made with care, homes beautifully decorated, women publishing books that are destined to be bestsellers. And there, before the day is even begun, I am defeated. I miss my babies. My refrigerator is messy and uninspiring. My house needs a good cleaning. And I know that once dawn comes, another day will pass without working on that book that is nearly fully written, but still remains only in my head. Ten minutes scrolling in the dark, and I have allowed myself to be defeated.

I am a mother with vast experience championing my children—hours and hours in the stands, behind the steering wheel, at the training table, in the sewing room. I put my whole heart into helping them along, giving them the tools and the support they need to succeed.

Can we be internet champions of other women, and of our own souls? Can we fight for, defend, support, encourage holiness? Can we do that? Can we make each other better, not by competing or complaining or comparing, but by coming alongside in love? With love?

If it beats up your soul to see someone's pictures day after day, if you compare your life to hers and—whether rightly or mistakenly—decide that yours falls short, if you envy, then tear out your eye. Or, stop going there online. Whichever works for you.

Don't keep tormenting yourself.

And when you go online, when you click there, go in grace. Go knowing that you are dearly loved by God Himself.

He doesn't care how many followers you have. Actually, He said, "Follow me." He isn't much interested in your selfies. He calls you to die to self.

He's not about platforms and personalities. He doesn't want you to use your friends for your glory. He wants to use your friendships to bring you closer to Him.

Go online to listen more than you speak. Assume the best of those whom you meet. Speak life and love into other women's hearts. Know that behind the perfect picture is a woman just like you—a woman who longs for friendship and camaraderie, a woman who might have had a very hard day. Be kind. Avoid snark like the plague it is. Don't mock your sisters who might not hold dear the same opinions that you do. And especially don't mock your husband or children. Some things are far too precious to throw out like so much litter along the information superhighway. Far, far too precious to be consumed by strangers.

When you go online, if you are moved to leave something behind, let it be something for the good. Let it testify to the best of you, the best of all of us. Let it nurture the people who read it, see it, remember you by it.

If you choose to scroll, glean the good, leave the rest, offer grace, and come away filled and not broken. But if you can't do that, until your soul heals, don't go there. Just walk away. Let yourself breathe freely without the barrage of information. Be a champion of your soul—fill it with nurturing thoughts. Crowd out those feelings of envy or insufficiency or failure.

Grant yourself space to stretch and grow without instant feedback.

Pull over to the side of the information superhighway. Have a picnic. See how the breeze blows warm and light when you aren't frenetically re-tweeting, responding, reacting. Just notice. Just listen. Just see what is right before you in real life. Take a deep breath. Take another.

Now follow Him.

Elizabeth Foss

TO PONDER WITH YOUR PEN

Instead of clicking through social media today, revisit this page in your journal. Here, record your stories. Here, see if you can capture your thought in the poetry of 140 characters carefully composed for God's eyes alone. Here, tell God what's on your mind. Stay away from the glare of the screen and keep your heart safely, completely, under His protection.

_____

_____

_____

_____

_____

_____

_____

_____

_____

_____

_____

_____

_____

_____

_____

_____

_____

LIFTED TO THE LORD

Yes, Jesus, I will follow You. Even in a world oriented to acquiring followers, I will choose instead to focus on being the one who follows. When I am distracted from Your will for me by wanting someone else's edited version of herself, please remind of Your vision for my unique life. And when I speak and if I lead in the world of social media, let it be from a place of servant-leadership, mindful of You, who knelt tenderly to wash the feet of Your followers.

THIRTY-FOUR *day*

JOB 12:7-10 (NRSV-CE)

But ask the animals, and they will teach you;
   the birds of the air, and they will tell you;
ask the plants of the earth, and they will teach you;
   and the fish of the sea will declare to you.
Who among all these does not know
   that the hand of the Lord has done this?
In his hand is the life of every living thing
   and the breath of every human being.

PSALM 96:11-12 (NRSV-CE)

Let the heavens be glad, and let the earth rejoice;
   let the sea roar, and all that fills it;
   let the field exult, and everything in it.
Then shall all the trees of the forest sing for joy

For further reading: Proverbs 8:22-31, Acts 17:28, Psalm 104: 31-35

THINK UPON THESE THINGS

After a week of fierce wind and rain, followed by two nights of freeze warnings, the day dawns bright, clear, and warm enough to be mistaken for a perfect May day. But it is early April. My soul and my body are weary. Winter was long and my to-do list just seems to grow longer. Contrary to any apparent common sense, I call a random "play day." Ignoring books, deadlines, and a growing pile of laundry, I gather my gaggle of children and we go to the woods. We hike a short path, flanked on either side by tiny white flowers we've grown to know as "fairy spuds," until we reach the large creek. And there, the entire world is blanketed by glorious cerulean flowers. It's bluebell season. We play in the creek and hike along its shores. We walk and talk with friends, throw sticks across the water, skip stones, and climb trees. I return home a different person—calmer, clearer, more peaceful—deep in my soul.

My soul is strengthened and soothed in nature. I come wired to know that God controls this vast creation and, in knowing that, I understand deep within me that God always bring order from chaos, whether it's dominion over the ocean or settling peace into my soul. Without words or even conscious thought, time in nature restores faith.

As I walk the path and notice the delicate detail of sweet bell-shaped flowers, I know I don't need to live in anxious tension. The same God who crafted every single perfect petal, can be trusted with the details of my life. I put myself in His hands and nothing on earth happens to me apart from His will.

God has shared His joy with the world through His creation. In Proverbs 8, we see that wisdom is with Him from the beginning—He created from a place of joy, delighting in the artistry of the world. Joy spills out onto a forest floor, exultant with gladness. God wants us here, here in His created world, entering into His joy.

We are more fully ourselves when joy is fundamental. In *Orthodoxy*, G. K. Chesterton writes, "Man is more himself, man is more manlike, when joy is the fundamental thing in him, and grief the superficial. Melancholy should be an innocent interlude, a tender and fugitive frame of mind; praise should be the permanent pulsation of the soul. Pessimism is at best an emotional half-holiday; joy is the uproarious labor by which all things live."

We look to the psalms for patterns of praise. There, we see that we are created to go forth praising God in nature (see Psalm 104:33-34). My soul comes fully alive on a spring day by the banks of Bull Run. In the lingo of the culture, this is "self-care," time outside in the natural world is a tool for restoration of well-being. The act of getting myself into the woods might be self-care, but the care itself is all God. Something supernatural comes over me if I only surrender to His carefully appointed place of respite. Nature nurtures my soul; the gentle restoration of my Creator softens the hard edges and fills the hollows and pits through the ministry of water, and sunshine, and flowers.

Elizabeth Foss

TO PONDER WITH YOUR PEN

Recall your favorite natural space, the place where your soul is always restored. Here, record that place. If you've got some time and are feeling verbally creative, write a canticle, praising the Creator for the place that soothes your soul. Or, break out the watercolors. Whether with words or pictures, go there with your fingers and go there in your mind. Then, as soon as you can, get outside and breathe deeply of His glory.

_____

_____

_____

_____

_____

_____

_____

_____

_____

_____

_____

_____

_____

_____

_____

LIFTED TO THE LORD

Sweet Jesus, I praise you for the restorative calm that comes when I spend time in nature. Please gently propel me outside. I know that calm usually settles upon me when I'm outdoors, but sometimes inertia overtakes me and I need a shove to get out and let nature nurture.

day THIRTY-FIVE

HIDE IT IN YOUR HEART

Today is a day to rest and be grateful. Take some time to look over your journaling from the week, to read a little more, to catch up on days when you didn't have as much time as you would have liked. Practice writing the memory verse here, and make it your own on the facing page.

Practice writing the verse here, and make it your own on the facing page.

PSALM 56:3 (NRSV-CE)

when I am afraid,
   I put my trust in you.

_____

_____

_____

_____

_____

_____

_____

_____

_____

_____

_____

_____

_____

when I
am afraid
I put my
trust
in you

PSALM 56:3

THIRTY-SIX *day*

PHILIPPIANS 3:8-11 (NRSV-CE)

More than that, I regard everything as loss because of the surpassing value of knowing Christ Jesus my Lord. For his sake I have suffered the loss of all things, and I regard them as rubbish, in order that I may gain Christ and be found in him, not having a righteousness of my own that comes from the law, but one that comes through faith in Christ, the righteousness from God based on faith. I want to know Christ and the power of his resurrection and the sharing of his sufferings by becoming like him in his death, if somehow I may attain the resurrection from the dead.

THINK UPON THESE THINGS

Halfway through my chemotherapy treatment, I was feverish, exhausted, and suffering from mouth sores that brought tears to my eyes when I swallowed. Physically and emotionally depleted, I could barely remember my former self. Instead of the anxiety I expected to overwhelm me before the upcoming scan to test whether the cancer had subsided, I felt nothing. It seemed as if I'd been in treatment forever, and in my weariness, I began to believe that my suffering was meaningless. I lost the motivation to persevere. Months earlier, I had wanted nothing more than to get well so I could care for my baby. But unable to tend to his basic needs or even hold him at times, I felt further detached from him with each passing day.

Then, days before my scan, a woman with the same cancer as mine died. Though I'd followed her blog since my diagnosis, I hadn't read it for several weeks, and I was shocked. I felt helpless, and needed to do something tangible. So, I wrote her name down and planned to remember her in prayer when I was scanned. As the scan approached, friends and family offered prayers, as they had done many times before. But for the first time, I asked how I could pray for them, too. I ended up with so many intentions that they filled multiple sheets of paper.

As I lay shivering on the cold machine, I shared the intentions with God. I was startled when the scan was over; a process that usually felt unbearably long had flown by. More remarkably, my thoughts hadn't once turned dark.

I continued taking prayer requests with me during the remainder of my treatment. The more pain I experienced, the more fervent my prayers became. It wasn't until I approached my last scan, five years later, that I realized how God had transformed my heart through this practice. By praying for others when I felt hopeless and lost, I had been given hope and a sense of purpose.

God sent His Son to suffer and die on the cross, in the ultimate act of salvific love. Jesus' suffering had meaning, and a purpose. He is the model for how we too can use our suffering to serve others—not just in moments of intense pain, but also in everyday annoyances and struggles. It can be jarring to hear Saint Paul say that he desires to share in Christ's sufferings, given how incredibly intense and numerous they were. But when we share in the suffering of Christ, we also share in the mystery of the resurrection—this is what Saint Paul had discovered. When we turn to God in our pain, He can draw life from what seems dead and goodness from what seems only bad. Knowing this, we can courageously seek communion with Jesus in our suffering, trusting that God's grace will fill the darkness of our earthly pain with the light of His glory.

Allison McGinley

TO PONDER WITH YOUR PEN

Sitting before a crucifix, make a list of all the pain you want to unite to Jesus' suffering. Nail your list to His cross (metaphorically speaking). Right next to that list, make a new one of the people for whom you are going to offer your suffering. Note their prayer intentions, their burdens, their sorrows.

_____

_____

_____

_____

_____

_____

_____

_____

_____

_____

_____

_____

_____

_____

_____

LIFTED TO THE LORD

Dear Lord, I offer to You my whole heart, including the places that are broken and bleeding. I ask You to allow me to enter into your suffering and to be consoled by Your Sacred Heart. Please bless me and bless the people I bring to You in prayer. Grant to us Your consolation and Your merciful care.

day THIRTY-SEVEN

PSALM 139: 13-16 (NRSV-CE)

For it was you who formed my inward parts;
   you knit me together in my mother's womb.
I praise you, for I am fearfully and wonderfully made.
   Wonderful are your works;
that I know very well.
   My frame was not hidden from you,
when I was being made in secret,
   intricately woven in the depths of the earth.
Your eyes beheld my unformed substance.
In your book were written
   all the days that were formed for me,
   when none of them as yet existed.

EPHESIANS 6:12 (NRSV-CE)

For our struggle is not against enemies of blood and flesh, but against the rulers, against the authorities, against the cosmic powers of this present darkness, against the spiritual forces of evil in the heavenly places.

For further reading: read all of Psalm 139

THINK UPON THESE THINGS

My daughter Karoline is a twin. Her sibling, whom she calls Benedict, died in utero. She is ten now and she talks about him frequently, with an intimacy and sureness that never fails to amaze me. What can we know of someone when we are tucked up together inside the darkness of a womb, in a place that is all our own, hidden from the rest of mankind? Despite personal observations of unique twin sensibilities, it is a sacred space that, for most of us, only God knows.

From the very first moment of our lives on earth, God has been with us in the darkness.

There is an intimacy in David's words in this psalm. He is so sure that God knows his very thoughts; God hears the words of his heart before they've been given voice. He is never, ever hidden from God. Even in the darkness. And there will be extended periods of darkness, just as there are extended periods of light. Perhaps the dark is precipitated by a series of unfortunate events. Or, perhaps, it's the dark night of the soul that settles when one feels the loneliness that comes with at once knowing God exists and feeling distanced from Him.

St. Teresa of Calcutta experienced prolonged bouts of profound feelings of abandonment. She confided, "Where I try to raise my thoughts to heaven, there is such convicting emptiness that those very thoughts return like sharp knives and hurt my very soul. Love—the word—it brings nothing. I am told God lives in me—and yet the reality of darkness and coldness and emptiness is so great that nothing touches my soul." Yet, she is remembered as a woman of cheerful service. How does one reconcile the darkness within in order to bear light to the world?

With that first dark night (and maybe with several that follow), it is entirely possible to stumble around futilely wondering why the Lord of light has abandoned you there. Those dark nights of the soul are pitched battles with forces of evil. In the black, in the pain, in the unrelenting questioning, the key to survival is to recognize that the times that are hard beyond imagination are not devoid of God.
God is there in the darkness. He's just as present as He is in the light. You don't have to know why it happened or how it ends or whether it's all going to work out in a way you consider favorable. You don't have to hear answers to your questions. But it is essential to keep asking the questions with the assurance that God knows the answers.

The psalmist begins with the affirmation that God has searched him and knows him, and he ends by begging God to search him and know him. He wants God to test his thoughts and to root out the sins. The God who knew us in the womb knew the pure soul who had yet to encounter the broken world. The God who knows us now can search our souls and help us root out those thoughts that hold us captive to anxiety and sorrow. He can shine a bright light of purification on the spiritual forces of evil.

He was with us in the darkness of the womb and He is here in this present darkness. We cannot survive unless we know God is with us in the black. Something slowly dies within us unless we can rest in the presence of God even in darkness. What is needed on our behalf is not the wit or the strength to find the switch and turn on the lights so that we can see Him. On the contrary, we can have peace in the darkness only when we learn to be still with Him in the dark.

Elizabeth Foss

TO PONDER WITH YOUR PEN

Keep asking the questions; keep wrestling with doubt before the throne of His infinite mercy.

_____

_____

_____

_____

_____

_____

_____

_____

_____

_____

_____

_____

_____

_____

_____

_____

_____

_____

_____

LIFTED TO THE LORD

Lord, my head knows that you are with me in the darkness.

Please, I beg You to persuade my heart of this truth.

day THIRTY-EIGHT

MARK 4: 3-9 (NRSV-CE)

"Listen! A sower went out to sow. And as he sowed, some seed fell on the path, and the birds came and ate it up. Other seed fell on rocky ground, where it did not have much soil, and it sprang up quickly, since it had no depth of soil. And when the sun rose, it was scorched; and since it had no root, it withered away. Other seed fell among thorns, and the thorns grew up and choked it, and it yielded no grain. Other seed fell into good soil and brought forth grain, growing up and increasing and yielding thirty and sixty and a hundredfold." And he said, "Let anyone with ears to hear listen!"

For further reading: Matthew 13: 3-9, Luke 8:1-5, and all of Mark 4:1-20

THINK UPON THESE THINGS

I am a wildly enthusiastic, though inconsistent, gardener. For nearly fifteen years, I've been planting a large organic garden, and for all those years, I've watched it be seized by weeds come mid-summer. A fruitful garden requires far more than a zealous spring start. Young plants must be nurtured: watered, thinned, and continuously protected from encroaching weeds. Almost daily attention is necessary. Every year, I promise I'm going to do better, but I fail again and again.

Worse than allowing my garden to grow out of control each year is my tendency to let my worries do the same. Just as weeds in a garden will smother young plants, my worries, given the freedom to do so, will overcome me.

As an agriculture major, I took a course in college called Weed Science. I learned there that the definition of a weed is "a plant out of place." The first step in control is recognizing the unwanted plant. Next, it must be removed. Most weeds are capable of spreading aggressively. They must be pulled and disposed of quickly so that their seeds don't end up in the soil, propagating an endless cycle of new weeds sprouting in your garden. You might consider that a worry is a thought out of place, and it must be plucked and burned, lest it multiply and shadow the thoughts that are oriented to what is good and right. Worries choke the good fruit. When we are worrying, we aren't trusting, and a relationship without trust is in trouble. Those rampant, negative thoughts essentially crowd God out in the same way that weeds in a garden prevent the sun from reaching tender, young plants.

I must be ever vigilant so that pernicious thoughts brimming with fear aren't able to creep in unrecognized. As I become more aware of negative thought patterns, my prayer is that trust in God will leave no space in the soil for worries. One of my favorite, simple prayers is, *Jesus, I trust in You.* Easy to remember, easy to utilize, to chant when necessary. The more I grow in trust, the less opportunity my worries will have to grow unchecked. Eventually, the ground cover of trust will be so great that my worries will shrivel underneath.

In the same way that I plant those tiny, life-filled seeds in the warming spring soil each year, God plants His seeds in each of us. I want the garden of my heart and mind to be free from worries, and open to trust, so that my life might bear fruit for Him.

Ginny Sheller

TO PONDER WITH YOUR PEN

Will you draw the garden of your soul today? Plot it out. What grows where? How do you make room for the things that matter? See that there is no intention to worry, no thoughts out of place taking up room in your soul garden.

LIFTED TO THE LORD
Jesus, I trust in You. Please increase my trust.

THIRTY-NINE *day*

PSALM 27:1-3 (NRSV-CE)

The Lord is my light and my salvation;
  whom shall I fear?
The Lord is the stronghold of my life;
  of whom shall I be afraid?

When evildoers assail me
  to devour my flesh—
my adversaries and foes—
  they shall stumble and fall.

Though an army encamp against me,
  my heart shall not fear;
though war rise up against me,
  yet I will be confident.

For further reading: read all of Psalm 27

THINK UPON THESE THINGS

I spent much of my young life living in fear. Fear of rejection. Fear of being poor. Fear of physical pain. You name the fear or the anxiety, I've experienced it. Probably more than once. It was in facing the greatest fear of my life that God broke through the dread surrounding my heart and brought me into the field of peace and grace, understanding fully how to trust and have confidence in His provision for me and my loved ones.

In September of 2014, my husband and I received devastating news. Our special-needs daughter Courtney was dying and the doctors had no more treatments to offer. After twenty-two years of daily seizures, her body was breaking down. We were told to bring her home and wait. After fighting so hard to keep her with us for all those years, our time together was now measured in weeks.

That first night home, I wept. I cried out to God at the injustice. In my head, I'd known this day was coming, but my heart couldn't bear the thought of never holding my daughter again. It felt like God had abandoned us.

I began to have nightmares that my daughter would die alone and in filth. That her dignity would not be honored, and we'd have to surrender her care to the state. I was losing the confidence and trust I'd had in the Lord's plan for my daughter's life. I was spiraling down into despair. Hope had disappeared.

After coming home from the hospital for the last time, I crumbled like Humpty Dumpty. I'd not slept in 48 hours. The list of Courtney's needs just kept getting longer and longer. My nightmares were coming true.

Exhausted and grieving what was coming, I fell to my knees next to my daughter's bed and wept. I begged God to help. *She's your daughter, too. How can you allow this to go on? You have to fix this.* My husband found me the next morning and gathered me into his arms to pray over me. He asked for God's protection and help.

As I listened to his prayer, the grip of fear squeezing the life out of me loosened. I was able to take a breath and began to speak the words with him. *"The Lord is my light and my salvation; whom shall I fear? The Lord is the stronghold of my life; of whom shall I be afraid? Be strong and take courage...we shall wait upon the Lord."*

Jerry continued to pray until Courtney woke up. For the first time since hearing about her imminent death, a glimmer of hope took shape in my heart. God would provide all we needed at the end of Courtney's life as he had throughout her life. What was required of Jerry and I was to wait upon the Lord and to love our daughter with all we had.

And so we did.

Those last months of Courtney's life were filled with countless miracles, spiritual and practical. Jerry and I prayed Psalm 27, the "Triumphant Song of Confidence of David," during those last days. Every need we placed before the Lord was met by family, friends, and strangers who heard of our story.

When the Lord called our daughter home, we knew we'd done *all* God had asked of us in loving and caring for Courtney. Just as David wrote in his song, God never left us. Not when we'd lost confidence and believed we were not as loved as others. Not when we feared what was to come. Not when Courtney died peacefully in our arms. After all, there was nothing to fear, God was always at our side.

Mary Lenaburg

TO PONDER WITH YOUR PEN

Here, now, commit to this paper and to the Lord, the thing you fear the most. Then, write the confident words of David over the words of your fears.

_____

_____

_____

_____

_____

_____

_____

_____

_____

_____

_____

_____

_____

_____

_____

_____

_____

LIFTED TO THE LORD

You know me, Lord. You know the fears that hide deep in my heart and you know the ones the bubble to the surface every day. Please infuse me with Your Spirit so that the confidence of God blankets my soul and smothers my fears.

FORTY

ROMANS 12:1-8 (NRSV-CE)

I appeal to you therefore, brothers and sisters, by the mercies of God, to present your bodies as a living sacrifice, holy and acceptable to God, which is your spiritual worship. Do not be conformed to this world, but be transformed by the renewing of your minds, so that you may discern what is the will of God—what is good and acceptable and perfect.

For by the grace given to me I say to everyone among you not to think of yourself more highly than you ought to think, but to think with sober judgment, each according to the measure of faith that God has assigned. For as in one body we have many members, and not all the members have the same function, so we, who are many, are one body in Christ, and individually we are members one of another. We have gifts that differ according to the grace given to us: prophecy, in proportion to faith; ministry, in ministering; the teacher, in teaching; the exhorter, in exhortation; the giver, in generosity; the leader, in diligence; the compassionate, in cheerfulness.

THINK UPON THESE THINGS

For the longest time, I thought to offer my body as a sacrifice, holy and acceptable to God, I had to offer it in service to others until it crumbled in exhaustion. Whether it was motherhood, friendship, or missionary service, I assumed God wanted to me to give all I had until there was nothing left of me.

I scoffed at the idea of self-care. *Where's that in the gospels?* I would think in a self-defensive haughtiness. That is until this definition of self-sacrifice and contempt for self-care sent me spiraling into a burnout crash of grand proportions.

Suddenly, the full context of Paul's words demanded my attention. This "living sacrifice" He calls us to make of our bodies is offered "by the mercies of God" as "spiritual worship." It "renews our minds" to rightly see the "good and perfect" will of God. I had long forgotten that my job was not to give everything away to others, but that it was to offer myself to God as a living sacrifice, giving my life here on earth to Him as spiritual worship. And to do so in the context of His great mercy, opening my eyes to see the goodness of His perfect will.

To offer ourselves as a living sacrifice to God is to accept that we cannot sustain constant self-sacrifice without renewal. In thinking I was above the need for self-care, I was losing perspective on my place in the body of Christ, thinking I could take on all the roles, rather than being a member, one among many. I was trying to give more than I had the grace to give and refusing to acknowledge that in stepping back to receive and be renewed, I was opening space in the body of Christ for other members to use their gifts and offer their own sacrifices as worship.

To present my body as a holy and acceptable sacrifice to God, it must first be living, and second be functioning as a member of the larger body. To keep going in physical service to others, and remain fully alive, my body must be nourished, nurtured, treated with kindness, offered mercy, and given rest.

When I accept that taking care of myself is actually a part of being transformed by Christ, I become a stronger member of the Body, and offer others the space to become stronger as well. As God transforms and renews my understanding of self-sacrifice and self-care as partners in His perfect will for me, I am beginning to see with new eyes the great beauty of the Body of Christ, which allows us space to be all that God calls us to be and doesn't demand more than we healthily can offer. What a beautiful grace to be one offering among many, the spiritual worship of my living sacrifice made more fully alive by the taking its place in the living, moving, breathing Body of Christ.

Colleen Mitchell

TO PONDER WITH YOUR PEN

Do you see self-care as a partner with self-sacrifice? Do you understand that to die for others is not to kill yourself? Spend some time thinking about the ways in which you honor that partnership between giving to others and nurturing yourself.

_____

_____

_____

_____

_____

_____

_____

_____

_____

_____

_____

_____

_____

_____

_____

_____

_____

LIFTED TO THE LORD

Dear Lord, strengthen in me the will to take good care of myself. Help me to see the practical steps I need to take to nurture the life you given to me. Show me, Lord, the people and the places that will support me as I endeavor to strengthen myself through tender care.

FORTY-ONE *day*

MATTHEW 6:34 (NRSV-CE)

"So do not worry about tomorrow, for tomorrow will bring worries of its own. Today's trouble is enough for today.

LAMENTATIONS 3: 22-26 (NRSV-CE)

The steadfast love of the Lord never ceases,
   his mercies never come to an end;
they are new every morning;
   great is your faithfulness.
"The Lord is my portion," says my soul,
   "therefore I will hope in him."
The Lord is good to those who wait for him,
   to the soul that seeks him.
It is good that one should wait quietly
   for the salvation of the Lord.

ISAIAH 40:8 (NRSV-CE)

The grass withers, the flower fades;
   but the word of our God will stand forever.

THINK UPON THESE THINGS

I see the frightened little girl tucked up under the covers, a *Children's Living Bible* open beneath the flashlight. Still, I marvel at the grace of those nights. It was my sister's Bible, given to her for her First Communion, an easily accessible translation, but she didn't want to read it. She gave the book to me to read to her, and then to read alone. I inhaled it, looking for answers to the questions that came in the absence of adult guidance. The Good Shepherd gave these words —this Word—to me, and they burrowed deep into my heart. Matthew 6 was a lifeline, a steady assurance that even if the next day was a chaotic mess at the hands of the grown-ups, God was in the moment, and God would provide the grace.

I see that girl a decade later, terrified in a hospital bed, the same words offered to her in song, the only way she could receive them then. *See?* He said, *I am unchanging. I am reliable.* And then I see her again, 20 weeks pregnant, in a bed surrounded by a gaggle of children, keeping very still, praying these words for a baby growing in a high-risk womb. *I'm still here. My promises hold true. I am with you forever.*

He shows me again and again that He is faithful. If only a battle could be won once and for all! But the enemy is cunning, and the serpent knows which form is most effective for his purposes. I still fear. Ironically, my greatest is fear is that the evil one will use anxiety to devour the very children for whom I prayed these verses.

Set apart from the rest of the Sermon on the Mount, Matthew 6:34 is formidable weapon in the war on pain. Suffering will always be a part of life. Sometimes, we cannot control the bad things that happen. But we intensify that suffering by dreading it, by turning it over again and again in our minds in anticipation of the next awful blow, by fearing the great unknown that is to come. Confronted with real burdens of today, we look beyond, to tomorrow, and we worry that we can't bear them then. God knew that this weapon of torture—this trick of the mind— would be used effectively, particularly against the most sensitive among us. Every blow of anxious thought would render us more receptive to the next one, the tender and broken skin of our souls prone to the infection of fear. With these verses, He speaks into those fears.

Jesus' words of wisdom on anxiety end with this final admonition, set apart for emphasis: take one day at a time. If we continue to worry about tomorrow, we quickly learn that there is always another tomorrow. There is always a future from which to borrow trouble. We have not yet received the grace He offers for that day; we don't yet know the gifts that wait there.

During that very difficult, very high-risk pregnancy, I was writing a book based on quotes from saints. I commented to my co-author that all these saints faced suffering with calm, faced death with happy resignation. I was on the strictest of bedrest, and I knew that my life was very much in danger, but every time I pictured the inevitable bloody delivery, I did not feel a sense of calm resignation. What was the secret to calm resignation? She pointed out that I was not yet to delivery, and I did not yet know if peace at the hour of death would be required of me when my baby was born. Maybe, she offered, grace is sufficient for the day, *when the day arrives*. Maybe total bedrest in a house of eight children was trouble enough for the present day.

Sure enough, the day of delivery arrived, six weeks earlier than predicted. It was a bloody mess. But my baby survived, and then, after a little while in the NICU, she thrived. And I didn't die. Further, I was definitely offered the grace and peace of an extraordinarily beautiful birth despite our high-tech, high alert surroundings. It was a surreal experience. In the moment, when all kinds of genuinely, objectively frightening things were happening, *He was there*. Just as He had always promised.

Do not fear. He is with you. Always.

Elizabeth Foss

TO PONDER WITH YOUR PEN

Just focus on today. For today alone, what do you want to bring before the throne of mercy? Where should God minister to your soul today?

Find each of these verses in your Bible. Underline them or highlight them. Make them yours.

LIFTED TO THE LORD

Dear Jesus, keep me in the present. Let me be acutely aware of today. Help me to see Your faithfulness, Your provision, Your blessing on just this day. As I consider it alone, apart from the days to come, give me the grace to notice the extraordinarily beautiful gift that it is.

day FORTY-TWO

HIDE IT IN YOUR HEART

Today is a day to rest and be grateful. Take some time to look over your journaling from the week, to read a little more, to catch up on days when you didn't have as much time as you would have liked. Practice writing the memory verse here, and make it your own on the facing page.

MATTHEW 6:34 (NRSV-CE)

"So do not worry about tomorrow, for tomorrow will bring worries of its own. Today's trouble is enough for today."

_____

_____

_____

_____

_____

_____

_____

_____

_____

_____

_____

_____

_____

_____

do not worry
about tomorrow
FOR TOMORROW WILL BRING
worries
of its own.
TODAY'S TROUBLE IS
enough for today.

MATTHEW 6:34

gratitude JOURNAL

DATE _____

_____

_____

_____

DATE _____

_____

_____

_____

DATE

DATE

DATE

DATE

DATE

DATE _____

_____

_____

_____

DATE _____

_____

_____

_____

DATE _____

_____

_____

_____

DATE _____

_____

_____

_____

DATE _____

_____

_____

_____

DATE

DATE

DATE

DATE

DATE

DATE _____

_____

_____

_____

DATE _____

_____

_____

_____

DATE _____

_____

_____

_____

DATE _____

_____

_____

_____

DATE _____

_____

_____

_____

DATE

DATE

DATE

DATE

DATE

DATE

DATE

DATE

DATE

DATE

DATE

DATE

DATE

DATE

DATE

DATE

DATE

DATE

DATE

DATE

THE TAKE UP AND READ COLLECTIVE

THE WRITERS:

Carly Magnolia Buckholz studied poetry at the University of Virginia before earning a Master's in Higher Education. She is from Burke, Virginia, but now calls Charlottesville home. Often next to a pile of books, Carly spends most of her time trying to convince her friends to read more poetry and baking scones. She enjoys writing about her family, rosemary, and the Blue Ridge Mountains.

Elizabeth Foss is the founder of Take Up and Read, a collective dedicated to inviting women to read, to ponder, and to respond to the Word of the Lord. A wife, mother, and grandmother, she's happy curled up with a good book or tinkering with a turn of phrase. Though she travels frequently, it's usually only between northern Virginia and her beloved Charlottesville, or to the weekend's dictated soccer or dance destination. Find her at www.elizabethfoss.com

Katy Greiner is a daughter, a sister, a recent graduate, and an aspiring teacher who's getting ready to face the real world. In that project, she's fueled by music, books, a strong cup of tea, good conversation, and hearing God laugh.

Mary Lenaburg is a writer, speaker, wife of 28 years and mother of two. She travels the country to share with groups of all ages about God's redeeming love, demonstrating that faith is the courage to want what God wants for us, even if we cannot see where the path leads. She continues to embrace her father's advice: "Never quit. Never give up. Never lose your faith. It's the one reason you walk this earth. For God chose this time and place just for you; so make the most of it." She can be found at www.marylenaburg.com

Allison McGinley lives with her husband and two kids in northern Virginia. When she's not dancing with her daughter or learning about Legos from her son, she writes, sings with a local worship band, and takes pictures of beautiful things. She shares her inspirational photography prints in her Etsy shop, "Be Not Afraid Prints."

Colleen Mitchell is a wife, mother, and foreign missionary. She is the author of *Who Do You Say You Are? Women Transformed by Christ in the Gospels*. Her second book is releasing this fall.

Ginny Sheller lives with her husband and eight children in Virginia. They keep bees, goats, and chickens and rarely have a clean house or a quiet moment. Ginny knits every day to maintain sanity, and shares her family's life in words and pictures on her blog, Small Things, www.gsheller.com.

OUR ARTISTS:

The book was designed by **Emma Catarino**. In her spare time, Emma loves to dance, read, hike, camp, try new restaurants, and spend time with her children and with friends. She loves music, and can often be found dancing around her kitchen. You can find her at www.emmacatarino.com.

Claire Craig, our calligrapher, is a freshman at Virginia Tech, studying Political Science. A dancer, candy enthusiast and lover of Christ, Claire spends her free time making music, working as a gymnastics teacher, and doing freelance artwork. Claire has an Etsy shop called Rooted in Love. You can visit her there at http://www.etsy.com/shop/RootedinLoveStudio.

The cover was painted and designed by **Kristin Foss**. Kristin is a self-taught watercolor artist who focuses on bright, detailed florals. With a paint brush in her hand and fresh blooms in a vase, she finds peace in God's Word while putting brush to paper. She lives in Los Angeles with her two daughters and husband, escaping to the beach and exploring the city. She enjoys creative cooking, thrift stores, nature walks, water and cotton.

Made in the USA
Middletown, DE
12 March 2021